Rightfully Yours:
How to Get Past-Due Child Support, Alimony, and Your Ex's Pension

by Gary Shulman

Self-Counsel Press Inc.
(a subsidiary of)
International Self-Counsel Press Ltd.

Printed in Canada.

First edition: 2002

Canadian Cataloguing in Publication Data

Shulman, Gary A.
    Rightfully yours: how to get past-due child support, alimony, and your ex's pension/Gary Shulman.

    (Self-counsel legal series)
    ISBN 1-55180-404-2

    1. Equitable distribution of marital property—United States.
2. Pensions—Law and legislation—United States. 3. Support
(Domestic relations)—United States. 4. Divorce settlements
—United States. I. Title. II. Series.
    KF523.7.S58 2002   346.7301'66   C2002-911361-X

Self-Counsel Press Inc.
(a subsidiary of)
International Self-Counsel Press Ltd.

1704 N. State Street	1481 Charlotte Road
Bellingham, WA 98225	North Vancouver, BC V7J 1H1
USA	Canada

√

Contents

SAMPLES

Notice

Laws are constantly changing. Every effort is made to keep this publication as current as possible. However, the author, the publisher, and the vendor make no representation or warranties regarding the outcome or the use to which the information in this book is put. This book is not a substitute for professional advice and cannot by its very nature address special problems or problems unique to individuals or the communities where they live. It is always best to consult licensed lawyers, accountants, and other professionals in your own community.

Dedication

I would like to dedicate this book to my lovely wife, Christine, whom I told I was writing a children's book about a fluffy squirrel named QDRO, and to my wonderful kids, Rachel, Nicole, and Eric. Hopefully, the millions of women in the US who have divorced or who are thinking about divorce will notice my commitment and passion for their plight—I also dedicate this book to them.

Preface

Any woman who has been divorced or is thinking about divorce must read this book. It can mean the difference between a lifetime of receiving pension benefits and child support income or receiving nothing. This book will make available to you the most powerful tool in collecting past-due child support and alimony without wasting thousands of dollars in legal fees.

This book focuses on two important issues: how to secure your share of your ex-husband's pension benefits earned during the marriage, and how to obtain past-due alimony and child support payments from your ex-husband's pension, profit-sharing, or 401(k) savings plan. It explains the best kept secret under federal law: the Qualified Domestic Relations Order (QDRO). By using a QDRO, you can secure your share of the pension benefits awarded to you at divorce. And you can tap into your ex-husband's retirement benefits for child support or alimony arrearages. Millions of divorced women are unaware of this powerful tool created by Congress in 1984 to help protect the financial rights of former spouses and children.

Unfortunately, many divorce attorneys are not familiar with QDROs and cannot provide appropriate guidance. Even worse, perhaps your own divorce attorney failed to prepare the necessary QDRO in your case. Remember that even if your divorce decree awards you a portion of your ex-husband's pension, profit-sharing, or 401(k) benefits, you will receive *nothing* unless a proper QDRO has been filed and accepted by your ex-husband's employer. And even if your attorney did draft a QDRO for you, did it include appropriate survivor language to protect your share of the benefits in the event of your ex-husband's death? Failure to include appropriate survivor protection in the QDRO is a common mistake.

A QDRO is the legal document necessary to obtain direct payments from your ex's retirement plan(s). If you were awarded a portion of your ex-husband's pension benefits or if he is currently delinquent in his child support or alimony payments, this book will be an invaluable resource. If you don't understand QDROs, you risk losing your rightful share of your ex-husband's pension benefits. Hundreds of thousands of women throughout the United States will discover to their horror that they will never receive the pension benefits awarded to them in their divorce decree or separation agreement because a QDRO was never prepared and implemented.

Throughout the United States today, there are millions of "dead-beat dads" who have refused to honor their child support or alimony obligations. This book will reveal how QDROs are the perfect vehicle for obtaining this past-due child support and alimony. Most employers, large and small, offer some form of pension or savings plan for their employees. If you think your ex-husband may participate in a pension or 401(k) savings plan, you can take immediate advantage of the federal QDRO laws and often you can get your past-due child support or alimony immediately in a single lump sum payment.

Even though QDROs have been around since 1984, these documents still confuse many in the legal community. As the country's leading authority on QDROs and as the author of four QDRO textbooks for attorneys, I felt compelled to write this book for divorced spouses to help them secure what is rightfully theirs. Whether you were granted a property interest in your ex-husband's pension benefits at divorce or are seeking to recover years of past-due child support or alimony payments, this book is for you. It's critical to your financial future that you understand the best-kept secret in the land — the QDRO. Through easy-to-understand examples, anecdotes, and model forms, I will take you on a step-by-step journey through the QDRO process so that you can recover your money now.

If you are an aggrieved husband whose former wife owes you alimony or child support, forgive me for my use of the female gender in most of my examples. Rest assured that you too can take advantage of the wonderful world of QDROs to recover past-due child support or alimony payments from your ex-wife's pension or savings plan. (I often use the male gender in this book to identify the "participant" and the female gender to identify the "alternate payee" because this usage represents the most common divorce scenario and minimizes the use of the cumbersome "he or she" and "his or her" writing style.)

CHAPTER 1

Did Your Divorce Decree Grant You a Portion of Your Ex-Husband's Future Pension? (It Should Have!)

You're in the middle of a bitter divorce. Well, it didn't start out that way, but now that the attorneys are involved, it's sure to end up that way. The attorneys are jockeying for position as they attempt to divide your marital assets. Just who will end up with that old gun collection, anyway? Who will be the lucky party that gets Aunt Ethel's original, hand-made Christmas ornaments? And let's not forget Poochie, your 12-year old, one-eyed Pekinese. As with all divorces, it seems that certain assets acquired during the marriage just seem to belong to your husband. It's almost a given. You know, the "manly" items, such as the gas grill, power tools, pool table, subscription to *Guns & Ammo*, and let's not forget that fine collection of remote controls. Of course, the wife usually gets to keep all of the cooking and cleaning supplies. After all, what's the husband going to do with these items? So, while he gets all the neat stuff, you end up with the Eureka vacuum cleaner, the Farberware, spice rack, and of course, Aunt Ethel's original, hand-made Christmas ornaments with a value placed at $10,000 by your husband's divorce attorney.

1. Don't Forget the Pension

While your attorney is racking up a bill at the rate of $200 to $400 an hour, it's no time to be penny-wise and pound-foolish. As the saying goes, don't sweat the small stuff. It may not be cost-effective to waste thousands of dollars in legal fees over the "stuff" that accumulated during the marriage, especially when the value of your husband's pension benefits is typically the largest marital asset. It may be many times more valuable than your home. That's right. Unknown to you, while your husband was giving you grief over the past 20 years (except for that one evening in June of '94 that sticks out in your mind), he was silently building a marital fortune through his pension benefits at work. At the time of his retirement, the pension benefits could be worth $500,000 or more.

Throughout the United States, the vast majority of large employers and even many smaller employers offer their employees some sort of retirement plan coverage. It could take the form of a 401(k) savings or profit-sharing plan, or it could be a pension plan that provides a monthly pension check for life on retirement. Many companies even sponsor more than one pension plan for their employees. For example, employees may be covered under both a 401(k) savings plan and a pension plan at the same time during their careers.

Before 1984 it was very difficult, if not impossible, for a divorced spouse to receive her marital rights to the pension benefits earned by the husband during the marriage. As a result, if your divorce occurred before 1984, it's very likely that your divorce decree did not mention your ex-husband's pension benefits at all. Both the decree and your separation agreement were probably silent on this issue. And even if the divorce court agreed that you were entitled to a portion of your ex-husband's pension benefits, it was still almost impossible for you to realize these benefits. Pension plan administrators were reluctant to send (and even prohibited by law from sending) former spouses a portion of the pension earned by their employees before 1984.

However, in 1984, a new federal pension law was enacted that made it much easier for former spouses to receive a portion of the pension benefits earned by their ex-husbands. These were referred to as the QDRO laws. Today, it's well-settled law that the pension benefits earned by your spouse during the marriage are considered *marital property* subject to equitable distribution on divorce. In essence, most domestic relations courts consider the nonparticipant spouse to be a *co-owner* of the pension benefits earned during the marriage by the husband. Beginning in 1984, former spouses of plan participants became eligible to receive their rightful share of the pension benefits *directly* from the plan administrator each month without having to rely on payments from ex-husbands. Imagine that. Upon the ex-husband's retirement, a former spouse could receive a pension check for life mailed directly to her home each month, just as if she were the plan participant. These new QDRO laws became part of the major federal pension law known as the Employee Retirement Income Security Act of 1974 (ERISA).

2. It's Your Property Right

If your divorce occurred after 1984, and your ex-husband was an *active* participant under a company pension plan or 401(k) plan, your attorney should have addressed this issue in your separation agreement or judgment entry of divorce. You *should* have been awarded a portion of your ex-husband's pension benefits that were earned (or accrued) during the marriage. Let me say this again. If your ex-husband was actively employed and covered under a company pension or 401(k) plan at any time during your marriage, you should be entitled, in your own right, to a portion of his eventual pension or savings plan benefits.

As a former spouse of a plan participant, you are considered to be a *co-owner* of the pension benefits earned during the marriage and do not merely stand in the shoes of a creditor. You should have been awarded a *property* interest in his pension benefits. The pension benefits earned during the marriage are just another asset to be "put on the table" when divvying up the marital assets, just like the toaster oven and the microwave. As one Ohio court said, "A pension plan is an investment made by both spouses during the marriage to provide for their later years. It's only equitable that each party enjoys their rightful share to half of the marital portion of the pension that accrued during the marriage."

Don't let your attorney forget about this very important pension asset. Many attorneys are very intimidated by QDROs and the federal pension laws and do not like dealing with pension issues during a divorce. But because more and more employees are covered by pension plans today, it should be of central concern to the attorney and the nonparticipant spouse.

It's also important to understand that your receipt of a portion of your ex-husband's pension payment is not automatic. Even if your divorce decree states that you are entitled to a portion of your ex-husband's pension benefits, you will never see any of these benefits unless a separate legal document called a QDRO was prepared by your attorney and submitted to the pension plan administrator for review and approval.

3. It's Not Alimony

Don't confuse your *property rights* with alimony or spousal support. When a domestic relations court grants you a portion of your ex-husband's pension benefits at divorce, it is merely assigning to you a piece of property that you already own. In the court's eyes, half of the pension benefits earned during the marriage are already yours. It just takes a QDRO to secure your property right. Your property interest in your ex-husband's pension is not considered alimony or spousal support. It belongs to you just as your ex-husband's share of the pension belongs to him. However, it is critical that your divorce decree include language that awards you a portion of your ex-husband's pension benefits. Even though the court considers you to be a co-owner of the pension, your share is not automatic by any means. If your attorney has not already done so, he or she should negotiate the division of your ex-husband's pension benefits during the divorce proceeding. Then your divorce decree or separation agreement should include language that expressly awards you a portion of his pension benefits. And finally, your attorney should prepare a QDRO for submission to your ex-husband's employer. This is necessary to secure your property interest in the pension benefits.

Any alimony or support payments (child support or spousal support) that may be granted to you at divorce are separate and distinct from the property rights granted to you at divorce. Unlike alimony or spousal support, which provides you with immediate and perhaps only temporary support after the divorce, you will generally not be eligible to receive your share of the pension benefits until your ex-husband is eligible to retire. But in many cases, depending on the type of pension plan involved, you can start receiving your share of the pension either immediately or before he actually retires. And your share of any defined contribution plan benefits (such as a 401(k) plan) can generally be paid to you immediately once the QDRO has been approved by the plan administrator.

4. How Much Is the Retirement Benefit Worth?

Before getting into a discussion of how much your spouse's retirement is worth, it is important to understand the distinction between the two basic types of retirement plans offered by companies today: defined contribution plans and defined benefit pension plans.

4.1 Defined contribution plans

The first type of retirement plan, and the simpler of the two, is called a *defined contribution plan*. Defined contribution plans come in many flavors. Some are referred to as 401(k) plans. Others are called profit-sharing plans, savings plans, or thrift plans. They all have one thing in common: a "pot" of money that is maintained for each plan participant and that grows each year with contributions and interest. By a pot of money, I mean that the company maintains an *individual account* for each employee. It's very similar to the individual retirement account (IRA) that one may open at a bank.

4.1.a Calculating the value of a plan

You can always calculate the value of a defined contribution plan by simply looking at the *total account balance* line on a plan statement. Typically, employees receive annual statements that show the current year's contributions and investment earnings and the end-of-year total account balance. The contributions to an employee's account under a defined contribution plan generally come from one of two sources. The first source is generally from the employee's own paycheck. In other words, your ex-husband may have elected to contribute a portion of his weekly paycheck to the plan. Usually, this is done on a *pre-tax* basis, which means that his contributions (the portion taken out of his pay-check) were distributed directly into his retirement plan account be-fore being taxed by Uncle Sam. The second source of contributions to a defined contribution plan comes from the employer itself. Your ex-husband's employer may make matching or voluntary contributions over and above those contributed by your ex-husband. The contribu-tions in the retirement plan are then generally invested in one or more available mutual fund alternatives (or in company stock, if applicable). Typically, employees can spread their contributions in any way they choose from among several investment alternatives, ranging from low-risk money market accounts to high-risk and more volatile types of funds.

At any time, the value of your ex-husband's defined contribution plan is merely reflected by the total account balance as of that date. For example, if you divorced on July 1, 1999, you should be entitled to half of the total account balance under your ex-husband's defined contribution plan that accumulated during the marriage until July 1, 1999. You, or your attorney, could obtain a financial statement from the plan administrator that shows the total account balance on that date. Assuming that your ex-husband did not participate in the plan before your marriage, you would simply be entitled to one-half of the total account balance on July 1, 1999. This "what you see is what you get" type of plan is fairly easy to incorporate into the marital estate during a divorce or dissolution proceeding. A professional pension evaluator is not needed for these types of plans. Again, a participant's benefits under a defined contribution plan are based solely on the amounts contributed to his accounts, plus any income, expenses, gains, and losses that may be allocated to his accounts. When participants retire or terminate their participation under a defined contribution plan, they can usually elect to receive their benefits in the form of a single lump sum distribution, payable immediately.

4.1.b What is vesting?

Perhaps you have heard the phrase, "He is only 40 percent vested under the profit-sharing plan." What does this mean? Most defined contribution plans have *vesting* clauses that apply to employer contributions. The word vesting refers to that portion of the employee's total account balance that he or she has *earned*. It's the amount that's *nonforfeitable* even if he or she were immediately to quit or retire. The portion of a participant's benefits that are considered vested cannot be taken away. For example, many 401(k) plans have a vesting schedule as follows: After one year of service, the employee may become 20 percent vested in the contributions made to his or her account by the employer. The next year, the employee will be 40 percent vested in those contributions; the year after that, 60 percent vested, and so on, until he or she becomes 100 percent vested after five years of service. If a plan participant quits employment after two years of service, when he is 40 percent vested, this means that he or she is eligible to receive only 40 percent of the value of the contributions made to the plan by the employer. The remaining 60 percent is lost and forfeited back to the plan. The amount that is lost is often referred to as a *forfeiture*.

A plan's vesting schedule, however, never applies to plan contributions made by the employee through voluntary payroll deductions. These employee contributions are always considered 100 percent vested. So, if your ex-husband elected to contribute a portion of his own paycheck to the plan, via convenient payroll deductions, he will always be 100 percent vested in his own contributions. These contributions can never be taken away from the employee or otherwise forfeited. Even if an employee quits after two years on the job, when he or she is only 40 percent vested in the contributions made by the employer, he or she will still be entitled to receive 100 percent of any employee contributions made to the plan during the two years of employment.

4.2 Defined benefit pension plans

The second type of retirement plan is called a *defined benefit pension plan*, a plan that pays out benefits in the form of a monthly pension check when someone retires. Unlike a defined contribution plan, such as a 401(k), generally no individual accounts are maintained under a defined benefit pension plan. This fact alone distinguishes it from a defined contribution plan. A defined benefit pension plan is merely a promise (albeit a contractual one) that the company makes to its employees to provide them with a monthly "pension check for life" once they retire. A participant's pension benefits are normally based on a plan formula that typically includes years of service with the company as well as the average salary earned by the employee during the final years of employment. A participant is generally not entitled to receive a lump sum distribution under a defined benefit pension plan. The benefits are typically payable only in the form of a "monthly lifetime annuity" starting when the participant retires, which ensures that the participant will receive a monthly pension check for the rest of his or her life.

Because account balances are not maintained for people under a defined benefit pension plan, it's difficult for employees and their spouses to get a feel for the true value of the plan. That's why benefits accrued by participants throughout their career under defined benefit pension plans are more of a mystery. That's why employees who are only 30 or 40 years old may know that they will someday be getting a pension check each month when they retire, but they cannot tell you how much it will be. Nor can they tell you how much their eventual pension is worth in today's dollars. And there's the rub. During a divorce, it's critical for a divorce attorney to attach a lump sum "value" to all of the marital assets, including the pension. While it's relatively simple to determine the value of a defined contribution plan simply by looking at the latest plan statement, it's a different matter entirely when it comes to your ex-husband's defined benefit pension plan.

For discussion purposes, when I use the words "pension plan" throughout this book, I am referring to a "defined benefit pension plan." The amount of benefits that a participant is entitled to receive under a pension plan is called his or her *accrued benefit*. Therefore, if an employee retires at age 65 with an accrued benefit of $2,000, he or she will receive a $2,000 monthly pension check for the rest of his or her life. Because no individual accounts are set up for employees under a pension plan, never use the words "account balance" when discussing your ex-husband's pension benefits.

Now, the all-important question. At your divorce, how much of your ex-husband's pension benefits are you entitled to receive as your marital share? The answer is not simple. Trying to determine how much a pension plan is worth is a difficult task even for attorneys. Quite often, divorce attorneys will hire an actuary or other pension professional to evaluate the pension. In order to evaluate your ex-husband's accrued benefit under the pension plan at the time of your divorce, the pension professional must figure out the "present-day lump sum value" of his anticipated future monthly stream of retirement income. Just knowing that your ex-husband has earned an accrued benefit of $800 per month (as calculated by his employer) at the time of divorce does not answer the question. Under a pension plan, a participant generally cannot receive his full, unreduced accrued benefit until he reaches the plan's normal retirement age (usually age 65). And even if you did know that his monthly accrued benefit was $800 when you divorced, what does this currently mean in terms of an immediate lump sum dollar amount? This is why it's necessary for the attorney to hire a pension professional. They must determine, in today's dollars, how much a future lifetime pension is worth. To do this, they incorporate such factors as mortality tables and interest rate charts.

Let's look at an example: Assume that John, age 45, has worked at an auto company for the last 20 years. Based on the plan formula, his accrued benefit is calculated to be $1200 per month. This means that if John were to quit his employment today, he would be eligible to receive $1200 per month for his entire lifetime, starting when he turns age 65. It is not a measure of how much he could receive immediately on termination of employment. Now, assume that you are getting a divorce from John today. Your attorney's pension evaluation expert would have to calculate how much John's future $1200 monthly accrued benefit is worth in today's dollars. This is called a *present value*. Based on actuarial statistics, which involves a lot of number crunching by the expert, his $1200 future monthly lifetime pension payments may have a present value of $120,000 today. Assuming that it's all marital (that his pension was earned entirely during the marriage), you would be entitled to $60,000 today, as your equitable ownership share of the pension.

5. The Use of Offsetting Assets

Many attorneys choose to use other nonpension-related assets when dividing the pension benefits of the husband. For example, if your husband's pension is valued at $120,000 at the time of divorce and you have equity in your home of approximately $120,000, perhaps the attorneys will work out a scenario in which you will get to keep the house and your ex-husband will keep his pension free and clear. However, because the value of the pension is quite often the largest marital asset, there may be no other offsetting assets to consider. In this case, your attorney must provide you with your own slice of your ex-husband's pension benefits. This is done through a QDRO (as explained further in Chapter 2).

6. A QDRO Is a Must

In order to secure your share of the pension, your attorney must prepare a QDRO and submit it to the pension administrator for review and approval. QDROs are fairly complex creatures in their own right, and the vast majority of divorce attorneys do not understand how to draft them. Without a properly drafted QDRO, you may never see any portion of your ex-husband's pension or 401(k) benefits, even though your divorce decree or separation agreement states in plain English that you are entitled to a portion of such retirement benefits.

♂♀

CHAPTER 2

What Is a QDRO?
(And Why Do You Need One?)

Repeat after me: "Q-D-R-O." Say it five times, fast: "QDRO, QDRO, QDRO, QDRO, QDRO." While your ex-husband is now yelling "STELLA," you should be yelling out the window at 4 a.m.: "QDRO!" Enough already. Why do you have to learn about this legal mumbo-jumbo when you're not an attorney? Well, most of you don't even realize that you already know some legalese. Take the word *alimony*, for example. In *Black's Law Dictionary*, it can be found between the words *Alimenta* and *A l'impossible nul n'est tenu*. It comes from the Latin *alimonia*, meaning sustenance, and stems from the common-law right of the wife to support by her husband. Most divorced spouses know what the word alimony means. But very few women have ever heard of a QDRO, which is short for Qualified Domestic Relations Order.

If your ex-husband, or soon-to-be ex-husband, worked at any time during the marriage for a company that had a pension plan or 401(k) plan, you had better become very familiar with the word QDRO. Similarly, if your "ex" now works for a company that sponsors a pension plan or 401(k) for its employees, this could be the gold mine that you have been waiting for if he owes you past-due child support or alimony. Your future economic security could depend on it. A few horror stories will help illustrate the point. If you decide not to read this entire book, make sure that you at least read the following three true stories. (Names have been changed to protect the ignorant.)

1. Horror Story No. 1

Take the case of Evelyn Schmidt. She had never heard of a QDRO either. In 2001, at the age of 62, she divorced David after a 30-year marriage. At that time, David worked for a large Fortune 500 company. He had been employed there for more than 25 years. Her divorce decree granted her 50 percent of David's pension and 401(k) benefits through his employer. That's right: the company has two retirement plans for David, not just one. One of them is a defined benefit pension plan that will pay him more than $3,000 per month for life when he retires, and the other is a 401(k) defined contribution plan. The pension plan is valued at $240,000. The total account balance in the 401(k) is $380,000.

According to the divorce decree that was entered by the court and signed by the judge, Evelyn was to receive half of David's future pension annuity that was attributable to the years of the marriage. This alone would have provided her with more than $1,400 per month from the pension plan for her entire lifetime. She was also awarded half of his 401(k) plan in the amount of $190,000, plus investment gains or losses until the date of actual distribution.

As it turned out, Evelyn's attorney never prepared a QDRO, even though her divorce decree granted her a share of the pension and 401(k) plan. In February 2002, David Schmidt died. The result? Evelyn will never see a penny from David's retirement plans. Why? One simple, but catastrophic answer. A QDRO was never prepared by her attorney and submitted to David's company for review and approval. After David's death, Evelyn quickly took a copy of her divorce decree to the plan administrator. She showed them the applicable section of her divorce decree, which clearly indicated that she was awarded half of her ex-husband's pension and 401(K) benefits. She even showed them the judge's signature on the decree. The plan administrator's response? "Sorry, but because we never received and approved a QDRO before your ex-husband's death, you are not entitled to any benefits from the pension or 401(k) plan." Does Evelyn have any recourse against her ex's company? Unfortunately, the answer is no. Her only recourse may be a malpractice suit against her attorney for failing to draft a proper QDRO in her case.

2. Horror Story No. 2

Mary Owens was divorced from Bob in 1991. In their separation agreement, Mary was awarded $100,000 from Bob's 401(k) plan through his employer. Mary thought that when Bob retired, she would receive her share of the 401(k) benefits from the plan. After all, the separation agreement was clear: $100,000 belonged to her. As the years went on after the divorce, Mary lost touch with Bob. She didn't even know where he lived. Sometime in 1998, Bob quit his job and, unknown to Mary, cashed-out his entire 401(k) plan. When Mary contacted the plan administrator in 1999 to inquire about her share of the 401(k) benefits, she was told that Bob had cashed-out the plan when he quit last year. When Mary said that she was entitled to $100,000 from the plan, she was told that no QDRO was ever submitted to Bob's employer for review and approval. As a result, when Bob applied for a distribution of his 401(k) benefits, the company had no choice but to pay Bob all of the benefits accumulated under the plan. Is Mary out of luck? Unfortunately, the answer is yes. Once the company made the total distribution to Bob in accordance with the terms of their own plan, it is certainly too late to submit a QDRO now. There are no more funds remaining in his account. A QDRO today would accomplish nothing. What are Mary's options now? She could sue her divorce attorney for malpractice for not preparing a QDRO in a timely manner. Alternatively, she could pursue Bob, either directly or through a lawsuit, to reclaim her share of the 401(k) benefits. Either choice could prove to be difficult and expensive.

If Mary had only heard of the term QDRO, she would be $100,000 richer today. And to make matters worse, she also found out that if a QDRO had been prepared when she divorced in 1991, the company would have given her the $100,000 right away. They would not have made her wait for Bob to retire — many companies like to cash-out alternate payees under QDROs as soon as the QDRO is approved, even though the participant is not yet eligible for a distribution. In this manner, they do not have to maintain separate records for alternate payees and trace investment gains or losses over a period of time. Imagine, if Mary had received her $100,000 in 1991 through a properly drafted QDRO and invested it, it could be worth more than $200,000 today.

3. Horror Story No. 3

Susan divorced Jim in 1997. As part of their property settlement agreement, she was awarded 50 percent of Jim's pension benefits through his employer starting when Jim retires. No QDRO was ever prepared and in 1999, unknown to Susan, Jim accepted an early retirement buyout offer from his company, which pays him $4,000 a month for life. He also elected to receive his benefits in the form of a single life annuity, which means that on his death, all benefit payments will cease. It wasn't until July 2002 that Susan found out about Jim's retirement years earlier. When she contacted the plan to inquire about her 50 percent share of the pension, she was told that no QDRO had ever been submitted to the company. Susan contacted an attorney to draft a QDRO today that would give her 50 percent of Jim's monthly pension benefits. Although it is certainly not too late to draft a QDRO (because Jim is still alive and receiving a pension), Susan will find out that certain restrictions are imposed on QDROs drafted after someone retires. For example, it is now too late for her to receive retroactive pension payments that date back to the time of Jim's retirement almost four years ago. Remember, had a QDRO been drafted in a timely manner when they divorced, Susan would have started to receive her share of the pension in 1999, when Jim retired.

But more of a loss is the fact that it is too late to provide Susan with a guaranteed lifetime of pension income. Because Jim had already retired and elected a single life annuity, Susan can only receive her share of the benefits for as long as Jim is alive and receiving a pension. Once Jim dies, Susan's share of the pension will also stop. Again, had a QDRO been prepared before Jim's retirement, it could have provided Susan with a pension for the rest of her life. Now, she can only hope that her ex-husband lives a long life so that she can continue to get her half of the pension.

4. Congress Created QDRO Laws in 1984

When Congress created the QDRO laws in 1984, its intent was to provide a vehicle for former spouses of pension plan participants to receive their rightful marital portion of their ex-spouse's pension benefits. After all, the pension was a marital asset subject to equitable distribution on divorce. So Congress decided that if the courts held that a former spouse was the co-owner of the pension, it was about time to provide a mechanism for companies to be allowed to pay a portion of a participant's pension benefits directly to a former spouse as called for in the divorce decree. Before QDROs came into existence in 1984, a plan participant's rights to his own pension benefits was paramount and untouchable. Once vested, the benefits were nonforfeitable. No one but the participant could receive the benefits. Not even creditors could go after a participant's pension benefits during a bankruptcy proceeding. ERISA's *anti-assignment* provisions prevented this. (ERISA, the Employee Retirement Income Security Act of 1974, is the federal pension law that was designed to protect a plan participant's pension benefits.) Participants could not assign a portion of their benefits to another party even if they wanted to.

In 1984, QDROs became the only exception to the anti-assignment provisions of ERISA. Now, for the first time, plan administrators were allowed to carry out the intentions of the divorce court. They were now permitted to divide the participant's pension benefits into two components and then send a portion of the pension directly to the former spouse without having to worry about their plans being disqualified by the Internal Revenue Service.

Because no QDRO was ever prepared in Evelyn Schmidt's case (see Section **1**. above), she can never receive any of David Schmidt's pension or 401(k) benefits, even though a portion of the benefits was deemed by the domestic relations court to be her own separate property right. This is because her ex-husband died before a QDRO was prepared. If he were still alive, it may not be too late to draft a QDRO now. See Chapter 15 for a discussion of options to consider if a QDRO was never drafted at the time of your divorce. Again, Evelyn's only recourse at this time might be a malpractice suit against her attorney. Had her attorney taken one extra step during the divorce by having a QDRO prepared for the sole purpose of securing a portion of David's pension benefits in accordance with the terms of her divorce decree, Evelyn's future economic outlook would be much brighter today.

These horror stories should illustrate the importance of QDROs. Unfortunately, however, hundreds of thousands of women across the country could find themselves in Evelyn's shoes one day. Are you one of them? Now that I have your attention, let's learn a little bit more about this very important legal document called a QDRO.

5. The Requirements of a QDRO

When the federal pension law known as ERISA was amended in 1984 to create QDROs, US Congressman Dan Rostenkowski of the Committee on Ways and Means said that:

> *the bill to amend ERISA would improve the delivery of re-*
> *tirement benefits and provide for greater equity under the*
> *private pension plans for workers and their spouses and*
> *dependents by taking into account changes in work pat-*
> *terns, the status of marriage as an economic partnership*
> *and the substantial contribution to that partnership of*
> *spouses who work both in and outside the home.*

For the first time, companies across America were required to honor a court order that qualified as a QDRO for the purpose of providing former spouses with a portion of their employee pension benefits.

The term Qualified Domestic Relations Order (QDRO) refers to a judgment, decree, or other court order that creates or recognizes the existence of an "alternate payee's" right to receive all or a portion of a plan participant's pension benefits. In other words, a QDRO is a special kind of court order that is signed by the judge and sent to the plan administrator for review and processing. The court, however, will not forward the QDRO to the plan administrator. This must be done by you or your attorney. Remember, the purpose of a QDRO is to make sure that when the time comes, the plan administrator sends you a check for your share of the pension or 401(k) benefits earned during the marriage.

Under a QDRO, you, the nonparticipant spouse, are referred to as an "alternate payee." Your ex-husband is considered the "plan partic-ipant." Although the best time to draft the QDRO is when you divorce, it is possible to draft a QDRO later, as long as your ex-husband is still alive. But to guarantee that you will get your share of a defined bene-fit pension for your entire lifetime, the QDRO must certainly be prepared and approved by the plan administrator before your ex-husband retires.

All of the information that must be included in a QDRO can be found in Section 414(p) of the Internal Revenue Code and in Section 206(d) of ERISA. Although the entire QDRO provisions of the law take up only several pages, they may as well be *War and Peace* as far as di-vorce attorneys are concerned. These several pages are very difficult for divorce attorneys to understand. Divorce attorneys are intimidated, and for good reason, by ERISA and the Internal Revenue Code. These documents read like Greek to most attorneys, because attorneys are like doctors: they often specialize in one area of the law, just as doctors specialize in one area of medicine. While it's true that good divorce attorneys will understand the critical need for a QDRO, they may not know how to properly draft one. This is because they are not pension or tax attorneys. But diligent divorce attorneys will hire an outside expert to draft the QDRO if they are not proficient at it, because they are well aware of the downside to not drafting the QDRO at the time of divorce. Divorce attorneys could leave themselves open to a potential malpractice suit years later if their clients never receive the rightful share of pension benefits awarded to them at the time of divorce. Hundreds of thousands of these time bombs are scattered across the country today, residing in attorneys' files. These are cases in which attorneys did not prepare the QDRO even though their clients were awarded a share of the participants' pension or savings plan benefits at divorce.

In order for a QDRO to qualify and be approved by the pension plan administrator, it must include certain legally required information:

- The name and last-known mailing address of the plan participant (your ex-husband)

- The name and last-known mailing address of the alternate payee (you, or your child in the case of a QDRO for child support purposes)

- The amount or percentage of the participant's benefits to be paid by the plan to the alternate payee

- The number of payments or the time period over which such payments are to be made to the alternate payee

- The specific name of the employer's pension plan

In addition, the QDRO must be:

- For child support, alimony, or property rights to a spouse, former spouse, child, or other dependent of a plan participant

- A court order, judgment, or decree signed by a judge in a domestic relations proceeding, such as a divorce, dissolution, or legal separation

6. Pension Plan Administrators Can Throw Out Your QDRO If They Don't Like It

A QDRO must include all of the required information in a manner that can be easily interpreted by the plan administrator of the pension plan. However, when Congress enacted the federal QDRO provisions of the law in 1984, they granted the power of reviewing and approving QDROs to the pension plan administrators themselves, rather than to the courts. As a result, most QDROs are rejected by plan administrators even though they have been signed by the judge. Imagine that. There are not many areas of the law where someone could look at a certified court order signed by a judge and respond, "Sorry, Judge, we don't like it. Try again." Because of these QDRO technicalities and the ability of the pension plan administrator to make the life of a divorce attorney miserable, many attorneys (perhaps even yours) are intimidated by QDROs and federal pension laws. And whether it's intentional or not, this is why many attorneys forget to draft QDROs in the first place.

Unless your divorce attorney is diligent in following through with the QDRO process (and most of them aren't), you will never see any portion of your ex-husband's pension benefits. For many attorneys, it's just a race to retirement: they hope they retire before the case they handled for you blows up (when your ex-husband retires and you find out that a QDRO was never prepared or approved by your ex-husband's employer). As adversarial as divorce attorneys are by nature, virtually every one in the country will agree to one thing: QDROs are, by far, their single, largest malpractice trap today. QDROs are their worst nightmare (which, unfortunately, could make them your worst nightmare as well).

If your attorney did draft a QDRO for you when you divorced, you must be sure that the QDRO was signed by the judge. But more importantly, you must be sure that the QDRO was reviewed and "approved" by the pension plan administrator, which is usually the company itself. Someone in the pension or personnel department may be responsible for reviewing your QDRO. Pension administrators are required by law to review a QDRO and alert the parties, in writing, of its qualified status. In other words, once your attorney submits the QDRO to the pension plan administrator, the company will respond to all parties and let them know whether it is approved or rejected. Therefore, it's important to follow through with the QDRO approval process. If you have not received a QDRO approval letter from the pension administrator, then you should contact the administrator to inquire about its qualified status. Don't rely on your attorney to follow through for you once he or she closes your file after the divorce. It would definitely be in your best interest to contact the plan administrator yourself if further changes are required to the QDRO.

It's also important to understand that if the pension administrator rejects the QDRO, it will not fix the QDRO for you. Unfortunately, it doesn't care if you ever submit a proper QDRO, because most companies don't like dealing with QDROs either. And some of them are very paternalistic toward their own employees. I heard one plan administrator remark: "Why should she get any of his pension while he spent thirty years up the pole and she was sitting at home eating Bon-bons?" What I am trying to say is, don't think for a minute that the plan administrator will help you get the QDRO approved. So I urge all of you not to give up on the QDRO if it was rejected. Contact the attorney who drafted it so that he or she can fix any deficiencies. And contact the plan administrator, repeatedly if you have to, to see if your QDRO was finally approved. Remember, unless your QDRO is approved by the plan administrator, you will not receive any of your ex-husband's pension or savings plan benefits.

CHAPTER 3

What Types of QDROs Are Available?

There are several kinds of QDROs; the styles are based on the type of retirement plan involved. And there are two basic types of retirement plans: defined benefit pension plans and defined contribution plans. A defined benefit pension plan pays a monthly pension check for life to a participant when he or she retires. A defined contribution plan, such as a 401(k) plan or profit-sharing plan, contains individual accounts for employees, who can receive lump sum distributions of their accounts when they terminate their employment or retire.

1. Two Types of QDROs for Defined Benefit Pension Plans

There are two types of QDROs for defined benefit pension plans. One is called a *separate interest* QDRO, and the other is called a *shared payment* QDRO. Under a separate interest QDRO, the nonparticipant spouse (the alternate payee) receives monthly pension payments that are *actuarially adjusted* to her own life expectancy. Because the monthly pension payments are tied to the alternate payee's lifetime, she will receive them for the remainder of her life once they commence. Under the shared payment QDRO, however, the alternate payee's share of the monthly pension payments are not actuarially adjusted to the alternate payee's lifetime. They remain based on the lifetime of the plan participant — the alternate payee simply "shares" in each monthly pension payment made to the participant once he retires.

Under a defined benefit pension plan, there are generally no individual accounts established for plan participants. Do not confuse defined benefit plans with 401(k) plans, which do maintain account balances for participants. Since there are no account balances, there are no interest or investment earnings. The pension plan merely pays a monthly pension check to the participant when he retires. These pension checks are payable for the entire lifetime of the plan participant. Before investigating more of the differences between a separate interest QDRO and a shared payment QDRO, it is important to understand a critical feature of all employer-sponsored pension plans: survivorship benefits, which determine what happens to participants' benefits when they die.

2. Survivorship Benefits under Defined Benefit Pension Plans

All defined benefit pension plans contain provisions for two types of potential survivor benefits in the event of the plan participant's death. One, a *preretirement survivor annuity*, pays a surviving spouse a monthly pension for life if the participant dies *before* retirement. In this case, if the participant dies while still actively employed (but after having met the plan's vesting requirements), the eligible surviving spouse will receive a preretirement *survivor pension*.

The second type of survivor annuity is called a *postretirement joint and survivor annuity*. This type of annuity, if elected by the participant when he retires, will pay a monthly survivor pension to an eligible surviving spouse if the participant dies *after* retirement. The good news is that former spouses of plan participants can receive survivor pensions under the federal QDRO laws to the extent that the QDRO includes this survivor protection for the alternate payee.

3. Former Spouses Can Get Survivor Protection

When Congress created QDROs in 1984, it made sure that former spouses of plan participants could get survivorship protection to secure their share of the pension benefits when participants died. As a result, the QDRO provisions of the law state that a former spouse (alternate payee) shall be treated as a current surviving spouse of the participant if the QDRO includes this survivor protection. Including adequate survivorship protection for the alternate payee is critical to any properly drafted QDRO. Knowing this, we can now discuss the two basic types of QDROs for defined benefit pension plans.

4. The Separate Interest QDRO

The term *separate interest* means that the former spouse will receive a separate *lifetime* interest in a portion of the participant's pension benefits. That is, once the alternate payee starts to receive her share of the participant's pension benefits, she will continue to receive them for the remainder of her lifetime. Of course, her share of the pension will be *actuarially adjusted* to her own life expectancy, which means that if she is younger than the participant, her share of the pension will be reduced to reflect her longer life expectancy. In this manner, the total value of the pension payable during her longer lifetime will be the same as it would be during the participant's shorter life expectancy.

Under a separate interest QDRO, because the alternate payee will receive her share of the benefits over her entire lifetime, there is no need to include *postretirement* survivorship protection for the alternate payee in the QDRO. However, *preretirement* survivorship protection is still necessary to protect the alternate payee's share of the benefits if the participant dies before retirement and before the alternate payee starts to receive her separate lifetime interest in the pension benefits. So when you think of a separate interest QDRO, think about preretirement survivor benefits only. (Sample 8 includes preretirement survivorship protection for the alternate payee. Section 8 includes the separate interest language providing the alternate payee with an "actuarially adjusted" lifetime pension.)

It is also important to recognize that under a separate interest QDRO, the alternate payee may elect to start her share of the benefits on or after the date on which the participant reaches the plan's earliest retirement age. This is true even if the participant decides to continue working. In other words, once the participant reaches the plan's earliest retirement age (say age 55), you may elect to start receiving your share of the pension benefits. But remember, if an alternate payee starts to receive benefits early (before the participant actually retires), the benefits may be significantly reduced to reflect the fact that payments are starting before the participant's normal retirement age (usually age 65). See Chapter 8 for a detailed discussion of the commencement date alternatives for an alternate payee under a QDRO.

5. The Shared Payment QDRO

Under the shared payment QDRO approach, the alternate payee's share of the pension is not actuarially adjusted to her own life expectancy. The pension stays based on the participant's life expectancy, and the alternate payee merely shares in the pension as long as the participant is alive and receiving a pension benefit. Under the shared payment approach, the alternate payee must wait for the participant to retire before she can commence her share of the benefits. Again, she simply shares in the participant's pension payments when he retires. Because the alternate payee does not receive an *actuarially adjusted* lifetime pension under the shared payment approach, the QDRO must include both preretirement and postretirement survivorship protection for the alternate payee to secure the alternate payee's share of the benefits if the participant dies either before or after retirement.

As you will see in Sample 9, Sections 9 and 10, it contains both preretirement and postretirement survivorship protection for the alternate payee. You will also see in Section 8 that the alternate payee must wait for the participant to retire before she can commence her share of the benefits.

6. QDROs for Defined Contribution Plans

When drafting a QDRO for a defined contribution plan, such as a 401(k) plan, you don't have to worry about separate interest versus shared payment QDROs. Those types are applicable only to defined benefit pension plans. There really is only one type of QDRO for a defined contribution plan — it essentially states how much of the participant's total account balance goes to the alternate payee. QDROs for defined contribution plans are much easier to draft and understand than are those for defined benefit pension plans.

See Samples 11, 12, and 13 for samples of defined contribution plan QDROs. The essential differences between these three models can be found in Section 7 of the QDROs. In Sample 11, the alternate payee simply receives 50 percent of the participant's total account balance as of the date of divorce.

∂♀

CHAPTER 4

Do You Need to Get an Attorney to Draft a QDRO? (What If You Can't Afford One?)

If you were awarded a portion of your ex-husband's pension benefits when you divorced (as part of the property settlement or separation agreement), you should first check with the attorney who handled your divorce to see if a QDRO was drafted for you at that time. If the answer is yes, you should then contact the pension plan administrator to inquire about the qualified status of the QDRO. In other words, you should see if the plan administrator accepted the QDRO. If no QDRO was ever drafted for you, or if the plan administrator rejected your attorney's draft of the QDRO, then you now have a new first priority. Get the QDRO drafted and approved right away. Failure to do so could result in your forfeiture of any pension benefits that were awarded to you in your judgment entry of divorce or separation agreement.

1. Contact Your Original Divorce Attorney

Start by contacting the same attorney who represented you during the divorce. Once you let him or her know that the QDRO issue was never finalized and that you are sitting in "limbo" regarding your property interest in the pension, it is possible that he or she will do whatever is necessary to secure your share of the pension. It's also possible that the attorney will do it free of charge in order to close this potential malpractice trap — especially if your account was paid in full when you divorced. Remember, your attorney should have handled the QDRO preparation for you when you divorced. Unless agreed otherwise, it was your attorney's duty to perform the necessary steps to secure your rights to the pension at the time you divorced — not later. It may be necessary for you to remind him or her of this fact.

2. Contact a New Family Law Attorney

If you don't get any satisfaction from contacting your original divorce attorney (or if you discover that he or she retired and opened a Starbucks), it may be in your best interest to find a new family law attorney to handle the QDRO drafting for you. You may have to interview several attorneys before you find one who is somewhat comfortable with QDROs (whether they draft QDROs themselves or outsource them to a QDRO expert). If you have moved away since the divorce, find an attorney in the same jurisdiction (county) where you were divorced. Because the QDRO document is a court order, it should be signed by a judge in the same jurisdiction where your divorce took place, and preferably by the same judge who handled your divorce case (if he or she still sits on the bench).

It may also be in your best interest from a cost perspective to shop around. If the attorney is going to charge you $1,000 or more to draft your QDRO, keep looking. The QDRO process should not be very expensive — perhaps $300 to $600. Don't be afraid to spend this money, though, if it means securing a lifetime of pension income. It's not a bad trade-off. In any event, you should beg, borrow, or, well, don't steal, to find the money to get the QDRO done. Every single day that you delay could be the day that your ex-husband either retires, quits his job, or dies. And if that happens, it could be too late for you to draft a QDRO. You will then receive none of the pension or savings plan benefits that were awarded to you in the divorce decree.

3. Try to Draft a QDRO Yourself Using a Sample QDRO from this Book

If you do not want to look for a attorney to draft your QDRO, do not be afraid to go it alone by using one of the sample QDROs included in this book. It's likely that the QDROs in this book are vastly superior to those used by many divorce attorneys. Most divorce attorneys are not familiar with the QDRO laws and will, perhaps in their own ignorance, rely on a QDRO template provided to them by your ex-husband's employer. You should understand that most companies do not care about your QDRO rights. Because of this, most model QDROs provided by the company itself are "plain vanilla" and often do not include many protective clauses that should be included in your QDRO. If you are somewhat reluctant to pursue QDRO preparation on your own, you may want to show your attorney the sample QDROs contained in this book — why pay him or her to do independent QDRO research, when it's right here in front of you? And by using the QDRO forms in this book, your legal fees could be substantially reduced. Remember one thing, however. I have drafted and reviewed more than 40,000 QDROs, yet even my QDROs are rejected from time to time. Do not be ovely alarmed if your QDRO is rejected. Stay diligent, and correct any deficiencies immediately on hearing back from the plan administrator.

Let's assume that your divorce decree included language that awarded you 50 percent of the total account balance in your ex-husband's 401(k) plan as of February 15, 2002 (your date of divorce). You could try using Sample 11 — which is meant to be used when assigning to an alternate payee 50 percent of the participant's total account balance under a defined contribution plan.

If you do attempt to draft the QDRO yourself by using one of the samples in this book, remember, a QDRO is really a court order that is signed by the judge. When typing the QDRO, you should have available to you a copy of your original divorce decree. All court orders, including your QDRO and your original divorce decree, must have a *caption* at the top of the first page of the order. The caption is the top part of the court order that includes the name of the case, the number of the case, the name of the judge, and the name of the order. Also, a vertical line of parentheses usually divides the left part of the caption from the right part. Be sure to include a caption at the top of your QDRO. You can use the same caption as was used in your divorce decree, but where it says "Decree of Divorce" or something similar to that on the right-hand side of the caption, you should include the words "Qualified Domestic Relations Order" to show that the document you prepared is a QDRO and not the original decree of divorce.

3.1 Step-by-Step Instructions for Completing a Sample QDRO Yourself

You don't have to be an attorney to complete the sample QDROs found in Chapter 19 of this book. Don't be afraid of some of the legal-sounding words or phrases found in the sample QDROs. Most individuals can understand a QDRO when they read it carefully. Following is a section-by-section description of Sample 11. Again, this sample QDRO is used for providing you with 50 percent of the account balance as of the date of divorce under a defined contribution plan.

3.1.a Section 1

Section 1 of the QDRO is considered *boilerplate*. That means it's a form of *legalese*. Just type it and forget about it. It simply states that the order is considered to be a QDRO in accordance with federal QDRO laws found in Section 414(p) of the Internal Revenue Code and under the federal pension law known as ERISA.

3.1.b Sections 2 and 3

Remember, in a QDRO, you are considered the "alternate payee" and your ex-husband, is considered the "plan participant." You should therefore complete Sections 2 and 3 of the QDRO accordingly. All QDROs must include the name and last-known address of the participant and alternate payee. If you do not know your ex-husband's current address, you should include his last known address. This should be acceptable to the plan administrator.

3.1.c Section 4

In Section 4 of the QDRO, you must include the actual (official) name of the company's pension plan or savings plan, as applicable. You can usually obtain this information by contacting the company's human resources or personnel department. You must get the name exactly right. If you leave out a comma or the word "Inc." from the name of the plan, this could give them a reason to reject your QDRO.

3.1.d Section 5

In Section 5, you should include the name of the state where you were divorced.

3.1.e Section 6

Section 6 of the QDRO simply states that it relates to the provision of "property rights" or "support" payments granted to you under the divorce. Again, this is considered boilerplate, which means type it and forget it.

3.1.f Section 7

The "guts" of the QDRO can be found under Section 7. This is where you include the "amount" of benefits payable to you. Sample 11 is already set up to provide you with 50 percent of the total account balance in the plan as of your date of divorce. Remember to include your date of divorce where indicated. This Sample QDRO also provides you with any interest or investment gains or losses attributable to your share of the benefits from your date of divorce to the date you receive your distribution.

3.1.g Section 8

Section 8 of the QDRO provides that you may receive your distribution as soon as the QDRO is approved by the plan administrator, to the extent permitted. If the plan does not permit you to receive your funds right away, the plan administrator will set up separate accounts in your name under the plan. You would then receive investment gains or losses on your share of the benefits until the date of distribution.

3.1.h Section 9

Section 9 of the QDRO gives you all of the rights granted to participants and beneficiaries under the plan. This is considered boilerplate language.

3.1.i Section 10

Section 10 simply states that if you die before you receive your distribution, then payments will be made to either your designated beneficiary or your estate. They will not revert to your ex-husband.

3.1.j Section 11

Section 11 protects you in the event of the death of your ex-husband before you receive your distribution. In essence, you will be treated as his beneficiary, to the extent of your assigned interest under the QDRO if he predeceases you.

3.1.k Section 12

Section 12 is just boilerplate. Type it and forget it.

3.1.l Section 13

Section 13 is also boilerplate. Under federal law, any amounts that you receive as alternate payee will be taxed to you. It's the law. You can't change it.

3.1.m Section 14

Section 14 is the "constructive receipt" section. This legal-sounding phrase simply means that if the plan administrator accidentally pays your ex-husband any of your money, he will be required to pay you back immediately.

3.1.n Section 15

Section 15 is legal boilerplate. "Continued jurisdiction," is a legal mechanism enabling you to go back to court, if necessary, to carry out the intentions of the QDRO, the parties, and the court if your QDRO is rejected.

3.1.o Section 16

Section 16 is boilerplate, too. If the company terminates the plan before you receive your distribution, this section will protect your benefits to the same extent that a participant's benefits will be preserved on termination of the plan.

3.1.p Section 17

Section 17 is called *anti-circumvention* language. This legal-sounding phrase is intended to protect you if your ex-husband takes any action that will limit or reduce the amount of your benefits under the QDRO.

4. Getting the Judge's Signature

Once you finish typing the QDRO, be sure to leave a signature line at the end of the order for the judge's signature. You now need to get it signed by the judge. You may have to contact an attorney for the sole purpose of running your QDRO through the court system (obtaining the judge's signature for you). However, some judges will sign the QDRO for you directly without requiring you to obtain an attorney. Contact the judge who handled your divorce by calling the courthouse, and ask to speak to the judge's clerk or secretary. If that judge is no longer sitting on the bench, you may contact any other domestic relations judge within that jurisdiction, or ask the courthouse receptionist to tell you who replaced your judge. You should then explain to the judge's clerk that you were previously divorced in that jurisdiction but that a QDRO was never prepared in your case. Next, ask the clerk if the judge will sign the QDRO if you send it to him or her. Be sure also to include a copy of your original divorce decree and separation agreement that shows that you were awarded a portion of your ex-husband's pension or savings plan benefits. When the judge sees that you really were awarded "x" amount of your ex-husband's pension benefits, he or she may sign the QDRO for you without the intervention of an attorney.

CHAPTER 5
How Do You Deal with the Plan Administrator?

Once a QDRO is prepared, it should be sent to the plan administrator for review and approval. In most cases, the plan administrator is the company itself. Your best bet is to send the QDRO to the attention of the human resources or legal department at the company where your ex-husband works (or worked). Not surprisingly, many plan administrators adopt a paternalistic attitude toward their employees, which may engender a combative attitude on the part of attorneys representing nonparticipant spouses. In seminars conducted for plan administrators, I have heard countless statements like "That might hurt our employee, if we give her that much of his pension" or "That doesn't seem fair to our worker."

Suggestions that plan administrators should avoid taking sides in domestic relations cases are frequently met with quizzical looks. This attitude can cause significant problems during the discovery process or when preparing a QDRO to secure the property rights of the alternate payee. The legal term *discovery* means the process of obtaining information from the plan administrator regarding your ex-husband's pension benefits. In other words, your attorney tries to discover all the pertinent information that will help him or her place a value on your ex-husband's pension or savings plan benefits.

1. Plan Administrators and You

Too many pension plan administrators view the nonparticipant spouse as an individual appropriating something that was earned through someone else's efforts. The economic partnership aspects of a marriage — the fact that a pension is deferred wages earned through the efforts of both parties and the contributions of the nonemployee to the overall marital estate — can be obscured by the misguided loyalty of plan administrators toward their employees. Many plan administrators do not realize that the nonparticipant spouse is actually considered a *co-owner* of the pension by domestic relations courts throughout the country. However, as unresponsive as some plan administrators are toward attorneys, they may be even less responsive to a former spouse trying to obtain information directly.

These attitudes may change once the QDRO is approved, because the nonparticipant spouse should be considered by the plan administrator to have the same status as a plan beneficiary and to be entitled to all of the required notices and other information sent to plan participants. Also, an alternate payee should then be permitted to receive information from the plan regarding the amount of the assigned benefits and how much the alternate payee would receive, depending on various potential commencement dates.

2. Remaining Nonadversarial with the Plan Administrator

When Congress created the QDRO laws in 1984, it granted plan administrators sole discretionary authority in approving your QDRO. Plan administrators come in all shapes and sizes. Some are rather sophisticated and have in-house ERISA (pension) attorneys and QDRO processing departments; others have never heard of ERISA or a QDRO. Many smaller companies are not aware of the QDRO provisions of the law and may use an independent third-party administrator to handle their employee benefits matters.

Whether you are dealing with a *Fortune 500* corporation like General Motors or a company like Lenny's Collision Center, both you and your attorney should treat the plan administrator in a kid-glove, nonadversarial manner. While this is next to impossible for many divorce attorneys, it is essential that you not antagonize the plan administrator when you submit a QDRO for review. It's a lose-lose situation if you do.

As the outsourcing QDRO review agent for many *Fortune 500* companies, I have received countless correspondences from attorneys that are submitting QDROs for review. Sometimes the cover letter to the QDRO will go something like this: "If you do not review this QDRO and make payment to my client within ten days of receipt, you will be held personally liable and I will make you a party to the case and start litigation immediately." This is not a good first impression to make on the plan administrator.

Even though your QDRO may be deficient from a strict legal perspective, a plan administrator may decide to go ahead and approve your QDRO by applying a liberal interpretation of it. The administrator may decide to make an assumption regarding a silent provision just to help the parties finalize the QDRO quickly. If you catch the plan administrator in a good mood, it may forgive some technical and non-substantive QDRO deficiencies that could otherwise result in a rejected order. For example, assume the QDRO awarded you $20,000 from your ex-husband's 401(k) plan but does not include language about where the $20,000 is to come from among your ex-husband's six investment accounts. If the company wanted to, it could reject your QDRO because the QDRO was silent on the issue of the allocation of your share of the benefits. It may say, "Sorry, your QDRO is rejected because it didn't tell us whether we should take the whole $20,000 from one of his accounts under the plan or on a *pro rata* basis from among all of his accounts." As ridiculous as this sounds, many companies reject QDROs everyday for this very reason.

If this is the only apparent problem with the QDRO, the plan administrator may assume that it was your intent to make a pro rata allocation, and approve the QDRO accordingly. However, if you or your attorney antagonize the plan administrator in some fashion, it would be well within its rights to reject your QDRO and require you to submit an amended order clarifying the method of allocation of benefits. This is just one of many examples of the importance of aligning yourself with the plan administrator rather than making an enemy of it. Not only could it apply stricter requirements when reviewing your QDRO, but it could also delay the review process for months or, in some cases, years.

Plan administrators who act in a clearly partisan fashion sometimes seem almost shocked and amused by the aggressive behavior of divorce attorneys. Sometimes administrators are downright hostile, and rude to boot. If they have suffered through incendiary phone calls from your attorney, requests to complete 40-page interrogatories, incessant letters demanding immediate responses, subpoenas, and hours spent in a witness waiting room, this may have fueled some of their hostility. Some plan administrators have received orders (purporting to be QDROs) that simply demanded a check for the alternate payee. Other plan administrators believe it is not their responsibility to school attorneys on drafting QDROs. Whatever the reason, you and your attorney need to exercise caution when dealing with plan administrators.

In some ways, plan administrators are similar to expert witnesses in court. They often answer you or your attorney's questions precisely, without providing additional information. For example, if you ask them to identify "all of the *pension* plans" under which your ex-husband is covered, they may say that he is covered under just one pension plan. What they may fail to tell you is that your ex-husband is also covered under the company 401(k) and the employee stock ownership plan (ESOP), which are technically not "pension plans." If you learn to ask plan administrators questions they can readily answer (avoid 40-page interrogatories) and never order them to do anything, the entire discovery and QDRO process can be sped up.

If the plan administrator takes a dislike to your attorney's efforts to qualify the QDRO, only you will be the loser. Plan administrators have a fiduciary obligation to review your QDRO in a prudent and timely manner, but they can and do let them sit for many, many months. Worse, if the QDRO is deemed deficient in some way, they are not obligated to tell you or your attorney what the deficiencies are. They may send you a one-sentence letter stating that the QDRO does not qualify and to please try again.

The importance of exercising good behavior in dealing with the plan administrator cannot be overemphasized. Your attorney's hardball tactics — useful and sometimes necessary in the courtroom — will fail when dealing with the plan administrator's review of a QDRO.

When you do confront plan administrators who are apathetic, overpaternalistic, or very adversarial, learn to bite your lip and keep your cool. Unfortunately, Congress, in its infinite wisdom, gave plan administrators nearly total discretionary authority over employee benefit matters relating to the domestic relations arena. The federal pension law known as ERISA, however, does provide participants and beneficiaries with certain rights regarding their benefits and information about them. But think of ERISA litigation only as your last resort.

3. Problems in Discovery

Providing the plan administrator with a reasonable amount of time to reply to your (or your attorney's) written requests for information and to review your QDRO will help with your relationship. Your attorney should be very cautious with his or her discovery approach. His or her requests for information may frequently be construed in a way that gives an unfair advantage to your ex-husband. Plan administrators have an uncanny ability to mold their answers to fit your questions. In other words, it's not what they say that can hurt you, it's what they don't say. Here are a series of examples that should aid you in understanding the need to exercise due diligence in the discovery process:

- The plan administrator is requested to identify the participant's current balance in the company savings plan. You are told that the participant has $4,000 in the plan. Unknown to you and your client, the participant took a $14,000 loan just days earlier.

- An auto worker's plan administrator is asked to calculate the participant's accrued benefit under the defined benefit pension plan. You and your attorney are told that he has accrued a pension of $957 a month. However, no one tells you that in one year, at age 49, he can retire at $990 a month for life, with an additional $1,050 monthly pension supplement until he reaches age 62.

- The administrator is asked to reveal all pension plans under which the participant is currently covered. Based on your attorney's discovery letter, you are informed that he is covered under a defined benefit plan that will pay $645 a month at age 65. The company does not reveal that he has a 401(k) savings plan with a balance of $23,000. Remember, your attorney only inquired about the "pension plan" and not about the savings plan.

- The plan administrator at the electrical workers "local 99" pension fund is asked to calculate the participant's accrued benefit. However, no one reveals that the participant is also covered by the electrical workers "national" pension fund as well. This means that he is covered under two separate defined benefit pension plans at the same time. He's covered under the *local* union pension plan and the *national* union pension plan.

- The company is requested to calculate a participant's accrued benefit. The written response indicates that no benefit is available because the participant has only been employed for four years. He has not yet satisfied the plan's vesting requirement. However, the participant has already worked there for four years and has started to accrue a pension, half of which may be marital. They don't tell you that he needs only one more year of service to become 100 percent vested in his accrued pension benefit. It is also well-settled law nowadays that a nonvested pension benefit does have value at divorce and should be considered when equitably dividing the marital portion of the pension benefits.

4. Your Rights under the Federal Pension Law Called ERISA

The Employee Retirement Income Security Act of 1974 (ERISA) entitles plan participants and beneficiaries to receive the following information regarding their plan benefits. Remember, once your QDRO is drafted, you, as alternate payee, have the same rights as a plan beneficiary to receive information from the plan. You are entitled to do the following:

(a) *Review plan documents*. All plan participants and beneficiaries can examine, without charge and during regular working hours, all plan documents, including plan contracts and copies of all documents filed with the US Department of Labor, such as detailed annual reports and plan descriptions.

(b) *Obtain a copy of plan documents*. All plan participants and beneficiaries can obtain a copy of all plan documents and other plan information by writing to the plan administrator's office. The administrator may make a reasonable charge for copies (usually not more than 25 cents per page).

(c) *Receive a copy of the plan's annual financial report*. The plan administrator is required by law to provide all plan participants with a copy of the summary annual report.

(d) *Receive an accrued benefit statement*. Upon written request, a plan administrator must furnish participants or plan beneficiaries with a statement regarding their rights to receive a benefit under the plan, and the amount of such benefits. The administrator must provide this accrued benefit calculation free of charge but is not required to recalculate it more frequently than once per year.

(e) *Receive a summary plan description*. One of the major obligations of a plan administrator is to furnish plan summaries (called summary plan descriptions, or SPDs) to all plan participants and beneficiaries. The purpose of the SPD is to provide a description of the key features of the plan in an easy-to-understand manner. It might be a good idea to request an SPD once your QDRO is approved. The SPD contains some information that may be of interest to you, such as early commencement reduction factors if you decide to start your benefits before your ex-husband's normal retirement age. It also includes all of the payment options from which you may elect to receive your benefits.

5. Administrative Fees for Processing QDROs

One gray area in the administration of QDROs by a plan administrator deals with fees charged to participants or alternate payees. Many companies today still charge an alternate payee for processing a QDRO in accordance with the requirements of ERISA and Section 414(p) of the Internal Revenue Code. Some *Fortune 500* companies request advance payment of $200 to $300 to accompany a QDRO before they will determine whether it qualifies.

The economics of dealing with QDROs can cause companies to increase expenditures to their attorneys, actuaries, and consultants for the review and processing of QDROs. But you might wonder whether administrative fees are fair, considering that plan administrators are required by statute to make qualifying determinations regarding QDROs. What can you do when the company's written administrative procedures dictate that a certain amount, a "QDRO processing fee," will automatically be deducted from their distribution? You will probably have as much success fighting city hall over a parking ticket.

Some clarification on this issue finally occurred several years ago in an official opinion letter from the Pension, Welfare and Benefits Administration (PWBA). The letter was prompted by a request from a plan administrator to permit the modification of the terms of its profit-sharing plan by allowing it to charge the account of a plan participant for any QDRO processing that affected this participant. In its opinion, the PWBA stated that an administrator of a retirement plan covered under Title 1 of ERISA may not charge an individual participant or an alternate payee any fees for processing a QDRO to determine whether it satisfies federal requirements for QDROs.

The rights of alternate payees under QDROs are guaranteed to them under ERISA and the Internal Revenue Code. To allow a plan administrator to charge for something it is required by law to provide flies in the face of equity. The PWBA did state that ERISA allows plans themselves to incur reasonable charges to cover certain costs and that plans may properly pay for reasonable administrative costs in processing QDROs. It distinguished between an alternate payee's rights to a portion of a participant's benefits as guaranteed by statute and an optional right that is permitted, but not required, under ERISA.

Occasionally, charges may be assessed to the participant or alternate payee. For example, a plan administrator may legitimately charge a participant for reasonable expenses incurred in exercising a plan option to allow employee-directed investments or loan processing fees for participants.

Despite the PWBA's opinion letter, some plan administrators are still charging participants and alternate payees QDRO processing fees. For example, if your QDRO used the separate interest approach, in which your benefits are actuarially adjusted to your own life expectancy, rather than remaining based on the life expectancy of the plan participant, it appears that the administrator may properly charge the participant or alternate payee for the necessary expenses incurred for hiring an actuary to perform this calculation.

At least one plan administrator circumvented this fee prohibition by charging only to review *draft* QDROs (those not yet signed by the judge). Attorneys were required to pay $250 for the review of a nonexecuted QDRO. The administrator failed to inform the attorneys that the fee would be waived if they submitted a QDRO already signed by the judge.

6. Constructive Notice of a QDRO

If your attorney is pursuing a QDRO on your behalf, he or she should send an immediate notice to the plan administrator (or even a first-draft, nonexecuted QDRO) to put it on notice of a pending QDRO. A nonexecuted QDRO is one that is not yet signed by the judge — it's still in draft form. Even if the draft QDRO is deemed not to be qualified, the plan administrator may still withhold the called-for portion to be payable to you pending the submission of a certified order. If your ex-husband is still actively employed, the company may flag his pension file to prevent him from making a sudden, premature distribution, loan, or withdrawal that would be detrimental to you. However, to really help secure your future rights to a share of the benefits, it is usually better to send a *certified* copy of the QDRO rather than a draft copy. A certified copy is one that is already executed by the court and shows the judge's signature. If a certified copy is sent, the plan administrator will be required to suspend or withhold the alternate payee's called-for portion of the benefits, even if the QDRO is otherwise deficient. This is especially important if your ex-husband is already retired or thinking about retiring in the near future.

7. The Company's Own Model QDRO Language

Many large employers have model QDRO language that they like to use to speed up the approval process. Generally, they are pleased to send you this information. Use this language wisely, however. Although it may expedite the approval process, their model language may not have your best interests in mind. Experience shows that it may be a good idea to have your attorney draft his or her own comprehensive QDRO language on the substantive and important issues and then to incorporate some or all of the company's nonsubstantive model QDRO language verbatim. This generally will help speed up the QDRO approval process. The plan administrator may appreciate the fact that you have succumbed, to some extent, to their total authority over QDROs.

Some plan administrators effectively try to dictate the terms of a settlement agreement and QDRO by forcing you to use their model language. They may refuse to even look at your QDRO unless it is based entirely on their fill-in-the-blank model language. Not only can this be dangerous, it is clearly an abuse of discretion on the part of plan administrators. The federal pension law, ERISA, does not give them the authority to dictate the terms of a QDRO. They must honor the provisions of a domestic relations order that satisfies the requirements for QDROs as they are set forth under ERISA and the Internal Revenue Code. In this situation, your attorney may have to pursue other avenues, ranging from contacting a director or vice president of the company to initiating an ERISA lawsuit for breach of fiduciary duty. The last approach is expensive and time-consuming.

On some issues, you should not bend. For example, assume that you were awarded 50 percent of the marital portion of your ex-husband's accrued benefit *as of his date of retirement* (using the traditional coverture approach, as discussed in Chapter 7). But many model QDROs prepared by companies permit you only to state your share of the benefit in the form of a fixed-dollar amount or as a percentage of his accrued benefit frozen as of the date of divorce. Remember that under a defined benefit pension plan, it may not be considered equitable to freeze your share of the benefits at divorce. Only the coverture approach will provide you with inflationary protection on your share of the benefits. If you simply fill in the company's own model QDRO with a fixed-dollar or percentage amount, it will freeze your share of the benefits. Your attorney may have to be assertive with the plan administrator on this issue by requesting, in writing, an explanation of why your language appears to violate ERISA regarding the provision of benefits to an alternate payee under a QDRO. He or she should also, if applicable, let the administrator know that under your state's well-settled case law, the coverture approach is the recommended approach for dividing benefits under a defined benefit pension plan.

On other issues, you may have to bite the bullet. For example, some plan administrators will not permit the alternate payee to receive her share of the benefits on an actuarially adjusted basis over her own life expectancy. In other words, they do not accept separate interest QDROs. Although the separate interest approach may benefit you, the administrator will probably not budge on this issue. However, be sure to include postretirement survivorship coverage in this case to assure you of a lifetime of benefits.

8. The Administrator's Approval and Signature

Many attorneys include signature lines at the end of the QDRO so that the plan administrator can approve and sign off on the order. If you want to expedite the approval process, eliminate this signature line. Generally, plan administrators will not sign a QDRO because they are not required to do so under ERISA or the Internal Revenue Code. Many plan administrators will deny a QDRO simply on this basis. They are required to abide by the terms of the QDRO and must furnish a written response indicating the qualified status of the QDRO. This response should sufficiently verify the QDRO's qualified status.

CHAPTER 6
Could Your Ex-Husband Have More than One Pension?

Often a participant will be covered under more than one retirement plan because many companies sponsor other qualified plans in addition to their defined benefit pension plans. Whether it is a form of defined contribution plan, such as a profit-sharing, 401(k), or thrift plan, or a stock plan such as an employee stock ownership plan (ESOP), remember to solicit this information from the plan administrator. It may also be wise for your attorney to depose the participant regarding all of his plans of coverage or, if the case comes to trial, to ascertain all of his plans of coverage on examination. Perhaps your attorney also had your ex-husband sign and notarize an Employee Benefits Entitlement Disclosure Form, which sets forth all of his plans of coverage, past and present, that may ultimately be considered to be marital property. It is always a good idea for your attorney to obtain this disclosure in writing; it is too easy to miss a pension plan when dealing with uncooperative plan participants and administrators. The written record will be essential proof of fraud or concealment in a motion to reopen the case.

1. Nonqualified Retirement Plans Not Subject to QDROs

Many companies also sponsor *nonqualified* retirement programs for certain eligible employees. These programs often supplement the company's standard retirement plans. Usually nonqualified plans are available only to highly paid employees. In other words, because of federal Internal Revenue Code pension restrictions for highly paid employees under all ERISA-governed plans, the company may establish a nonqualified plan to make up the lost benefits for its highly compensated employees. These nonqualified executive compensation plans should be considered in the same light as an ERISA-qualified plan when equitably dividing retirement benefits on divorce. But because nonqualified plans are not governed by ERISA, you cannot use a QDRO to divide these nonqualified benefits. Many plans will not even honor any type of court order to divide these benefits. This does not mean that the nonqualified benefits are not marital; it simply means that the company will not pay you your share of the nonqualified pension benefits directly.

Your attorney should have addressed the issue of your ex-husband's nonqualified benefits at the time of your divorce. These benefits should have been considered when valuing and equitably dividing his total retirement package. If the company in question will not accept a court order to divide this benefit directly, you should still be entitled to half the marital portion of these benefits that were awarded to you at the time of divorce. Many attorneys include language in the judgment entry that requires the participant to pay his former spouse directly when he goes into pay status. As he receives his check each month from the nonqualified plan(s), he must send his former spouse the called-for portion in accordance with the terms of the judgment entry of divorce.

2. Types of Defined Contribution Plans

There are many types of defined contribution plans, but they all have one thing in common: individual accounts for each plan participant. The various names for defined contribution plans include the following:

- 401(k) plan
- Profit-sharing plan
- Retirement savings plan

- Thrift plan
- Employee stock ownership plan (ESOP)
- Savings investment plan (SIP)

Generally, the word "savings" in the name of the plan is an indication that your ex-husband is covered under a defined contribution plan, and this increases the likelihood that you can receive an immediate lump sum distribution on approval of a QDRO. That is because most plan administrators do not want to maintain separate accounts for alternate payees over the years. They would just as soon cash you out and be done with it. In fact, quite often, you can receive your distribution under the defined contribution plan before your ex-husband is even eligible to receive benefits himself. When you or your attorney contact the plan administrator, be sure to ask the administrator if it sponsors any type of defined contribution plan for its employees. Don't simply ask if it has a 401(k) plan. It may answer "no" if it refers to its plan as a "profit-sharing" plan.

3. Types of Defined Benefit Pension Plans

The various types of defined benefit pension plans include the following:

- Final average pay plan
- Career average plan
- Hourly pension plan
- Cash balance plan
- Money purchase pension plan

If your ex-husband is covered under a defined benefit pension plan, this generally means that someday he will receive a monthly pension check for life. Usually no individual account balances are maintained under a defined benefit pension plan. A participant's accrued benefit is based on a plan formula that often incorporates his or her final average pay and years of service. In other words, the company may figure the average of the participant's earnings over the last five years of his employment, when his or her earnings are, of course, highest. This final average pay will then be multiplied by the participant's years of service and perhaps another percentage multiplier. As you can see, the longer people are employed and the more money they make, the larger their pension benefits. Some companies average the participants' earnings over their entire working career rather than just looking at the final five years of earnings. This approach is referred to as a *career average plan*, which often results in smaller pension benefits because the participant's earnings were much lower 15 or 20 years ago.

If your ex-husband works as an hourly employee, his pension benefits may be based on his years of service and on the *benefit level* in effect on his date of retirement. These are often easy calculations. For example, if the benefit level is $20 per year of service and your ex-husband worked for 20 years before retiring, his monthly pension will be $400 per month. Under a defined benefit pension plan, his accrued benefit is generally payable on a monthly basis once he retires and continues for his entire lifetime.

There is one exception to the general rule that defined benefit pension plans do not contain account balances for plan participants. Many companies sponsor a *cash-balance* pension plan for their employees. This plan is a kind of hybrid between a defined benefit pension plan and a defined contribution plan. Although it is technically considered a defined benefit pension plan because the benefits accrue based on a pre-determined formula and participants can receive monthly pension benefits for life, individual accounts are established for each plan participant. But don't get the wrong idea: this is not the same as a 401(k) plan. The amount of money appearing on the participant's account statement at any point in time is somewhat of a phantom balance because if the participant were to quit, he or she would not necessarily be entitled to 100 percent of those funds. Usually, the account balances are converted into a monthly pension benefit at retirement. But nonetheless, a QDRO for a cash balance plan should look a lot more like a QDRO for a defined contribution plan. The QDRO should refer to a percentage of an "account balance" and it should also apply "interest credits" to the alternate payee's share of the account balance just as he or she would be entitled to investment earnings under a 401(k) plan from the date of divorce to the date of distribution.

4. Coverage under Two Defined Benefit Pension Plans

Watch out for simultaneous plans of coverage! Again, many companies have both a defined benefit pension plan and a defined contribution plan for their employees. Participation in both plans is generally automatic. This means that participants are accruing benefits under both plans at the same time. However, in some instances, a participant may be covered under two defined benefit pension plans at the same time.

It is not unusual for a union employee to be covered under more than one defined benefit pension plan at the same time. Usually one of the plans is sponsored by his *local* union, whereas the other is sponsored by the *national* branch of the union. A good example is an electrical worker who is covered by both his local union pension plan and the National Electrical Benefits Fund (NEBF).

Many attorneys lose sight of this fact. Upon divorce, the nonparticipant spouse should be entitled to half the marital portion of *each* of these two pension plans and a separate QDRO should be drafted accordingly for each one. It is important to remember that the local union plan is generally not administered by the same folks that handle the national union plan. This is why two QDROs are required. And because there isn't a "one-size-fits-all" QDRO, you may find out that your QDRO for the local pension plan was approved while the same QDRO language was rejected by the national union's pension plan. As frustrating as this may be, you have to handle each QDRO separately and treat each plan administrator as though they are different companies.

5. A Separate QDRO for Each Plan

If you were awarded a portion of each of your ex-husband's retirement plans, a separate QDRO should be prepared for each plan. This is especially true if one is a defined benefit pension plan and the other is a defined contribution plan. Many attorneys make the mistake of drafting a single QDRO when two plans are involved. They believe that if they simply reference the name of each plan in one QDRO, that the alternate payee's rights will be secured with respect to each plan. Most plan administrators will reject a single QDRO in this instance. Remember, the structures of defined contribution plans and defined benefit pension plans are significantly different. One refers to account balances, interest earnings, and lump sum payments, while the other refers to accrued benefits, actuarial adjustments, and monthly lifetime pension checks. For these reasons, a single QDRO cannot work. If you want to speed up the QDRO approval process, you or your attorney must draft a separate QDRO for each type of plan.

However, if your ex-husband participates in two defined contribution plans with the same employer, such as a 401(k) plan and an ESOP, it is possible to combine these plans into a single QDRO. This is because each plan is of the same type — each contains individual account balances for the participants and the QDRO terminology is the same.

6. Don't Forget about Your Ex-Husband's Previous Employment

Nowadays, it only takes about five years for an employee to become fully vested in his pension benefits. This means that once the employee has worked at the same company for five years, he will have a nonforfeitable right to a future pension benefit. It is possible that your ex-husband may be entitled to a *deferred vested* or *terminated vested* pension benefit from his previous employer. Typically, these deferred vested pensions do not start until he reaches the plan's normal retirement age, usually age 65. So, if your ex-husband worked at more than one company for any length of time, you or your attorney should investigate whether he earned a vested pension right from his previous employer. If so, you should be awarded a portion of these benefits if they were earned, in part, during the marriage.

σ♀

CHAPTER 7

How Much of the Pension Are You Entitled to Receive?

In order to help you understand how much of the pension benefits you should be entitled to, this chapter will introduce a couple of new concepts. As a result, it may be the most difficult chapter to understand in the entire book, but to help you obtain the best possible pension rights under your QDRO, it's valuable reading — even if you have to read it twice.

Generally, when dividing a participant's pension benefits upon divorce, the goal of the divorce court is to provide you with 50 percent of the "marital portion" of your ex-husband's pension benefits. The term *marital portion* means that portion of his pension benefits that were earned during the marriage. This amount may be simple to determine under a 401(k) savings plan, but it can be very difficult to calculate under a defined benefit pension plan. Before we get into some of the difficult concepts of dealing with a defined benefit pension plan, let's first look at how one would calculate the marital portion of a defined contribution plan.

1. Determining the Marital Portion of a Defined Contribution Plan

It's relatively easy to draft a QDRO for a defined contribution plan, such as a 401(k) plan or a profit-sharing plan. Because the benefits consist of a "pot" of money (the total balance under your ex-husband's accounts), the task is simply to determine how much of the pot is yours. This amount is usually governed by the terms of your divorce decree or separation agreement. Many decrees will include language such as "Wife is entitled to 50 percent of total account balance at time of divorce," or perhaps a dollar amount is already stated in the decree. The QDRO then must be drafted to follow the terms of the decree. But generally, if you were married the entire time of your ex-husband's participation in the plan, you should be entitled to 50 percent of the account balance at the time of divorce, plus any interest earnings or losses attributable to your share of the account balance until the date of distribution. You could then use Sample 11 for this purpose.

2. Premarital Account Balances

If your ex-husband was employed by the company before you were married, perhaps he already participated in the plan on the date of your marriage. In this case, he would have a *premarital balance* when you married. This is usually considered a nonmarital asset. In other words, you would not be entitled to any of the account balance that he already had accumulated in the plan when you married. If this is the case, your share of the amounts accumulated during the marriage would be determined by subtracting the total *premarital* account balance on the date of your marriage from the total account balance on the date of divorce. You would then be entitled to half the amount that accumulated during the marriage. A word of caution, however. When a participant does have a premarital account balance earned before the marriage, some courts also exclude the growth (interest earnings) that accumulate on the premarital balance during the marriage when determining the marital portion of the benefits.

3. QDRO Tips for Determining Your Share of a Defined Contribution Plan

Here are a few tips to help you determine your share of a defined contribution plan.

3.1 Interest and investment earnings

Remember to include language in the QDRO that provides you with any interest or investment gains or losses that are attributable to your share of the total account balance. In other words, if the QDRO provides you with $50,000 as of the date of your divorce, you should also be entitled to any interest earnings on the $50,000 from the date of divorce to the date of your total distribution. Don't leave this issue up to the plan administrator. Make sure that your QDRO states that you are entitled to any interest or investment gains or losses attributable to your assigned share of the benefits until the date of distribution.

3.2 Sneaky plan loans by participants

If your ex-husband knows that a QDRO is forthcoming, he may run into the plan administrator's office and request a loan from his 401(k) plan. This is especially true if the QDRO provides you with a percentage of his total account balance. Consider the following example. Nicole was in the process of obtaining a divorce from Bill in late 2002. Bill knew that Nicole's attorney was in the process of drafting a QDRO to give Nicole 50 percent of Bill's total account balance under the plan. Because the total account balance at that time was $100,000, Nicole would receive $50,000 from the QDRO. However, unknown to Nicole, Bill applied for a loan from his 401(k) plan just one month before the divorce was final. He received a loan for $40,000, leaving his remaining total account balance at $60,000. Therefore, when the plan administrator interpreted the QDRO prepared in Nicole's case, which provided her with 50 percent of the account balance as of the date of divorce, they gave her just $30,000 rather than the intended $50,000. If your attorney drafted a QDRO for you, be sure that it includes language, if applicable, which states that your share of the total account balance should be "calculated without regard to any previous loans taken by the participant." In this manner, Nicole would still have received $50,000, as if no loan were ever taken.

3.3 Contributions made after divorce that were for periods before divorce

Under a defined contribution plan, the alternate payee usually receives half the participant's total account balance at the date of divorce. Typically, she is not entitled to any contributions made to the plan after the divorce. Many QDROs are drafted in this fashion. They simply state that the alternate payee is entitled to 50 percent of the participant's total account balance at the date of divorce, period. Consider the following example. Rachel gets divorced from Eric on December 12, 2001. On that date, Eric's total account balance under his 401(k) plan was $84,000. Many attorneys would simply draft a QDRO that provides Rachel with half this sum, or $42,000. However, unknown to both Rachel and her attorney, the company did not make its 2001 plan contributions until sometime in the year 2002 for tax purposes. On February 15, 2002, the company contributed $6,000 to Eric's account for the year 2001. Technically, because the divorce occurred on December 12, 2001, Rachel should have been entitled to a portion of the contributions that were really made for the 2001 plan year. Therefore, she should be entitled to a portion of the $6,000 contribution even though this contribution was not made until sometime in 2002. It is a good idea to include language in the QDRO that provides that the alternate payee is entitled to a pro rata share of any plan contributions made *after* the date of divorce but that are attributable to periods *before* the divorce. Had Rachel's QDRO included this language, she would get almost $3,000 more under the QDRO.

4. Determining the Marital Portion of a Defined Benefit Pension Plan

Now we are getting into the difficult portion of this chapter. There are many ways to define an alternate payee's share of the benefits under a defined benefit pension plan. Some attorneys use a percentage of the participant's accrued benefit at the time of divorce. Others include a fixed-dollar assignment of benefits. In any event, the QDRO should always refer to the participant's "accrued benefit as of a particular date." Remember, a pension plan is not like a 401(k) savings plan. Because typically no individual accounts are maintained for plan participants under a defined benefit pension plan, never refer to a participant's "account balance" or "investment gains or losses" when drafting the QDRO. The date to use for the calculation of the participant's accrued benefit should be the date of retirement, not the date of divorce.

Generally, a participant's *accrued benefit* can be calculated at any point in time during his working career. The accrued benefit is usually payable in the form of a monthly pension for life, starting at the participant's normal retirement age (usually age 65). Many attorneys who represent the plan participant attempt to draft a QDRO that *freezes* the alternate payee's share of the benefit at 50 percent of the participant's accrued benefit under the plan "as of the date of divorce." While a plan administrator will certainly accept this language (and may even recommend it in one of its model QDROs), this wording can be extremely hazardous to the financial health of the alternate payee. This is another good reason for an attorney who represents you not to arbitrarily use the company's own model QDRO. A company provides model QDROs for one reason only: to expedite the QDRO review process. And from a paternalistic standpoint, it does not really care whether the alternate payee's rights are secured in an "equitable" manner.

When drafting a QDRO, the task of determining the portion "earned during the marriage" becomes a key issue. This chapter discusses the recommended approach to dividing benefits under a defined benefit pension plan. I believe there is generally one approach to follow when drafting a QDRO for a defined benefit pension plan: the coverture approach. The purpose of the coverture approach is to provide the alternate payee with *inflationary* protection for his or her share of the participant's pension benefits.

The question of inflationary protection for the nonparticipant often arises because you too may have to wait for years to receive your share of your ex-husband's pension benefits. Unfortunately, some courts simply believe that all postdivorce salary increases are nonmarital. This essentially freezes the nonparticipant's share of the pension as of the date of the divorce. This would be tantamount to freezing the nonparticipant's share of a 401(k) plan as of the date of divorce and providing 100 percent of the future interest and investment earnings (even those attributable to the nonparticipant spouse's share of the benefits) to the participant.

No attorney in the country would argue that the nonparticipant spouse is not entitled to her own interest and investment gains or losses attributable to her assigned share of the "pot of money" under the 401(k) plan. Yet many attorneys for plan participants will vehemently oppose any attempts to provide growth protection to an alternate payee under a defined benefit pension plan. Let's not forget that you are actually a co-owner of the pension in the eyes of the court.

The equitable goal of the parties and the court, all other things being equal, should be to calculate the marital portion of the participant's benefits earned during the marriage and then equally divide this amount between the participant and nonparticipant spouse. Therefore, before one can determine the amount payable to the alternate payee, the marital portion of the pension must be calculated. Again, many attorneys who represent plan participants like to base the alternate payee's share of the pension on his or her frozen accrued benefit at the time of divorce. But it certainly does not make sense to calculate your 50 percent share of the marital portion of the pension based on your ex-husband's accrued benefit calculation as of the date of divorce, while his 50 percent share of what should be the same marital portion is based on his ultimate pension at retirement.

Co-owners of an asset should not be treated in this fashion. It's inconceivable that so many attorneys have gotten away with shortchanging the rights of the alternate payee for so long — and it's almost a crime that they can still get away with this in some courts today. What we have here is concrete proof that the wonderful world of ERISA and pension plans is overly complex and often misunderstood by domestic relations attorneys and judges.

5. Coverture: The Recommended Approach for QDROs under Defined Benefit Pension Plans

The recommended approach for dividing pension benefits is known as the *coverture approach*. It provides the nonparticipant spouse with a proportional share of the participant's final accrued benefit calculated as of his date of retirement. Under a defined benefit pension plan, unlike a defined contribution plan, such as a 401(k) or profit-sharing plan, a participant is promised a future, projected retirement benefit that typically commences at the participant's normal retirement age. This benefit is calculated in accordance with a plan formula that often incorporates years of service, final average salary, or, if it is an hourly plan, the benefit level in effect as of the participant's date of retirement. The employer then makes regular, annual contributions to the plan during its employees' working careers in accordance with actuarial projections of the sums needed to fund such future promised pension benefits.

Because future projected accrued benefits are promised under a defined benefit pension plan, the plan bears the investment risk even if the fund is short. For this reason, neither contributions nor interest are typically posted to individual accounts in a defined benefit plan.

Therefore, the only equitable way to protect the alternate payee against future inflationary trends during the years before the commencement of benefits is to structure the alternate payee's share of the benefits in the QDRO on the participant's ultimate accrued benefit at retirement rather than on his or her accrued benefit calculated at the date of divorce.

The country's leading experts in the field of present values and QDROs may refer to their recommended method of dividing pensions under a defined benefit plan by different names, such as the coverture approach, the marital portion approach, and the proportionate share approach, but they are all based on identical methodology.

As I state above, a participant's accrued benefit is generally based on the plan formula in effect on the date of retirement, which typically incorporates the participant's final average salary and a specified plan formula percentage. Once the applicable percentage is applied to the average salary component of the plan, the product is then multiplied by the participant's total years of service under the plan to determine his or her final pension benefit. Therefore, from a mathematical standpoint, the benefits actually accrue in equal increments for each year of service under the plan. That is, each and every year of service (even those earned during the marriage) are multiplied by the same formula amount.

An example should help illustrate this point. After working for the ABC Equipment Co. for 30 years, Jay is preparing to retire at age 65 at the end of 2002. He is covered under a defined benefit pension plan. The annual accrued pension is calculated by multiplying his years of service by his highest three-year average salary. This product is further multiplied by a 1.8 percent factor to produce his final pension amount. His pay for the three-year period prior to retirement is anticipated to be: $45,000 for 2000, $48,000 for 2001, and $51,500 for 2002. His final average salary is determined to be $48,166.67 ($45,000 + $48,000 + $51,500 = $144,500 divided by 3 equals $48,166.67). His annual pension will be $26,010 (30 years of credited serviced x 1.8% x $48,166.67). Or, stated another way, his annual pension will be the product of $867 (1.8% x $48,166.67) times 30 years of service. As you can see, the amount of $867 derived from the plan formula is applied to each and every one of his 30 years of service (even those years earned during the marriage).

5.1 The mechanics of the coverture approach

To best represent your QDRO rights, your attorney should utilize the coverture approach for dividing benefits under a defined benefit pension plan. Under this approach, you are entitled to 50 percent of the marital portion of your ex-husband's accrued benefit under the plan as of his date of retirement, when his pension is, of course, greatest. Under this approach, however, you do not simply receive 50 percent of your ex-husband's ultimate retirement benefit. Once his final benefit is calculated at retirement, the "marital portion" is determined by multiplying his final pension by a "coverture fraction." The numerator of the coverture fraction is equal to his years of service earned under the plan during the marriage, and the denominator is equal to his total years of service earned under the plan as of his date of retirement. You would then be entitled to 50 percent of the marital portion of the ultimate pension.

The use of the coverture approach is the only way to provide an alternate payee with inflationary protection on her ownership share of the pension. Under this approach, the numerator of the coverture fraction remains constant. That is, if your ex-husband earned ten years of service under the plan during the marriage, the numerator would always equal ten years, regardless of how many years he continues to work after the divorce.

The denominator of the coverture fraction represents your ex-husband's total years of service under the plan as of his date of retirement. Therefore, as he continues to earn additional years of service after the divorce, the denominator continues to grow by one each year. In reality, as the denominator grows by one each year while the numerator remains constant, your fractional ownership interest in his pension (the coverture fraction) is actually decreasing each year — 10/11ths, 10/12ths, 10/13ths, etc. If he retires after 30 years, the coverture fraction would end up being 10/30ths. This annually decreasing coverture fraction is continually applied to a larger pension as the participant's accrued benefit continues to grow with each additional year of service after the divorce. In essence, with each passing year after the divorce, you are earning a smaller and smaller percentage of a larger pie, as his pension grows. This is how an alternate payee receives her growth protection under a QDRO for a defined benefit pension plan.

This coverture approach is widely recommended as the only means of providing inflationary protection for an alternate payee under a defined benefit pension plan. The Ohio Supreme Court, in 1990, said:

> *In determining the proportionality of the pension or retirement benefits, the nonemployed spouse, in most instances, is only entitled to share in the actual marital asset. The value of this asset would be determined by computing the ratio of the number of years of employment of the employed spouse during the marriage to the total years of his or her employment.*

With respect to addressing the alternate payee's co-ownership interest in the participant's pension utilizing the coverture approach, an Ohio Appellate Court said it best:

> *Because the ultimate value of a pension benefit, and of the respective shares of the spouses, increases with the number of years of service credit, an argument is frequently made that a former spouse is unjustly enriched when the value of his or her share is increased by post-divorce participation in a plan by the other spouse.*
>
> *… a retirement plan is an investment made by both spouses during marriage to provide for their later years. They anticipate that the value of the investment will increase with time. At divorce, each spouse is entitled to the value of his or her investment. When the investment has not yet matured, each is entitled to its value at maturity in proportion to the years of marriage. The nonemployed former spouse is not entitled to share in the direct contributions made by the participant former spouse after divorce. However, the nonemployed former spouse is entitled to the benefit of any increase in the value of his or her unmatured proportionate share after divorce attributable to the continued participation of the other spouse in the retirement plan. That increase was contemplated when the investment was made. It would be inequitable to deprive the owner of its value. So long as each former spouse is limited to his or her proportionate right to share, there is neither unjust enrichment of the nonparticipant nor an inequitable deprivation of his or her rights.*

In viewing the nonparticipant as a co-owner of the pension, this Ohio court logically found that the co-owner of an asset must be allowed to share in the inevitable growth of that asset.

The equitable approach to use in the vast majority of circumstances when dividing pension benefits under a defined benefit pension plan is the coverture approach. This approach recognizes how benefits are calculated under defined benefit pension plans, and then calculates the proportionate share upon which the alternate payee's benefits are based. The beauty of the coverture approach is that it virtually always provides a fair and equitable distribution of benefits under a defined benefit plan, regardless of which party an attorney is representing (participant or nonparticipant spouse).

5.2 Model coverture language

When drafting a QDRO using the coverture approach, you may use the following language, as applicable:

> ***Amount of Alternate Payee's Benefit:*** *This Order assigns to Alternate Payee an amount equal to the actuarial equivalent of **Fifty Percent (50%) of the "Marital Portion" of the Participant's accrued benefit** under the Plan as of the Participant's benefit commencement date, or the Alternate Payee's benefit commencement date, if earlier. The Marital Portion of the Participant's accrued benefit shall be determined by multiplying the Participant's accrued benefit by a fraction (less than or equal to 1.0), the numerator of which is the number of months of the Participant's participation in the Plan earned during the marriage (**from [date of marriage] to [date of divorce]**), and the denominator of which is the total number of months of the Participant's participation in the Plan as of the earlier of his date of cessation of benefit accruals or the date that Alternate Payee commences her benefits hereunder.*

The coverture language stated above is really not as complex as it looks. It merely instructs the plan administrator to calculate your share of the pension on your ex-husband's accrued benefit under the plan at the earlier of his actual date of retirement or the date that you elect to start your benefits under the QDRO. Once the plan administrator calculates the accrued benefit, it will multiply the benefit by the coverture fraction to calculate how much of it is considered "marital." Then it will multiply that amount by 50 percent to determine your half of the marital portion of the pension.

5.3 If your divorce decree did not include a coverture formula

If your divorce is still pending, be sure to mention this coverture formula approach to your attorney. He or she may not be familiar with it. It is the best approach to use to define your share of your ex-husband's pension benefits, but only under a defined benefit pension plan. If your divorce is already final, the QDRO will have to be drafted to follow the terms of your divorce decree. Many attorneys will simply include a single sentence in your divorce decree such as "Wife gets 50 percent of Husband's pension benefits" or "Wife gets half of the marital portion of the Husband's pension." These vague phrases could cause a problem when drafting the QDRO. But because they don't preclude you from receiving growth protection on your share of the pension, it is not unreasonable to assume that the intent was to use a coverture formula when drafting the QDRO. This should certainly be your argument. But sometimes the divorce decree will include a statement such as "Wife to receive 50 percent of the Husband's accrued pension benefit calculated as of the date of divorce." If your decree reads similar to this, the use of a coverture formula could be more difficult. Remember, under the coverture approach, your share of the pension is based on your ex-husband's final pension benefit at retirement and not on his accrued benefit at divorce. But if the language in your decree implies that it is based on his pension at the time of divorce, you could be stuck in to preparing a "frozen" accrued benefit QDRO.

In any event, don't agree too quickly to the use of a frozen-benefit approach in the QDRO. It may be worth having your attorney reopen your case to push the coverture argument in court. This approach is widely recommended throughout the country, and spending a few dollars today on a new court hearing could provide you with a much higher pension benefit for life when the time comes to start the pension.

CHAPTER 8

When Can You Start Receiving Your Share of the Pension? (Do You Have to Wait Until Your Ex Retires?)

If you were awarded a portion of your ex-husband's pension benefits under a defined benefit pension plan, you may be permitted to commence your pension benefits before your ex-husband retires. A separate interest QDRO may include language stating that you will start receiving your share of the pension benefits once your ex-husband reaches the plan's earliest retirement age. This is true even if he decides to keep working. Remember, a separate interest QDRO is one that provides you with your own separate lifetime of pension income that is adjusted to your life expectancy. If you already have a QDRO in place, be sure to check the language to see if it allows you to start receiving your benefits early. Most QDROs drafted by attorneys today do use the separate interest approach.

Once your QDRO is approved by the pension plan administrator, you may contact it to find out the earliest date you can start to receive your share of the pension. Most pension plans have a normal retirement date of age 65. That is the age at which a plan participant can retire and receive full pension benefits. Most pension plans include early retirement provisions that permit employees to retire before the age of 65; many offer employees the opportunity to retire at age 55 or 60. However, quite often, the benefits received at early retirement are reduced to reflect the fact that the participants are starting the benefits before their normal retirement age. The term *actuarial reduction* is often associated with an early retirement benefit. This means that the participants' benefits will be actuarially reduced for each year that their early retirement date precedes their normal retirement date. For example, let's assume that John is age 60 and his accrued benefit is $2,000 per month. This means that he could quit work today at age 60 and receive a monthly pension of $2,000 per month starting when he turns age 65. But this plan has an early retirement provision, which states that he can retire at age 60 and receive an actuarially reduced pension starting right away. Rather than waiting until age 65 to start his full $2,000 per month pension, he could start receiving a pension now (at age 60), but he would receive only $1,300 per month. This $700 per month reduction in benefits reflects the fact that he will be receiving his pension earlier and over a longer period of time.

1. The Early Retirement Subsidy

For some employees considering early retirement, the whopping actuarial reduction to the pension is not worth it. Many employees decide not to retire early (at age 55 or 60) because they don't want to incur a 40 percent or greater reduction in their monthly pension benefits. Enter the early retirement subsidy. In our example above, John's pension was reduced from $2,000 per month to $1,300 per month for life. His company's pension plan does not offer an early retirement subsidy to its employees. But if John worked across the street at Acme Tools, he could retire as early as age 60 and receive his full accrued benefit under the plan. This is because the pension plan sponsored by Acme Tools includes a *full* early retirement subsidy for any employees who elect to retire on or after the age of 60 but before their normal retirement age of 65. In other words, if the participants' age 65 accrued benefit is $2,000 per month, they could elect to retire at age 60 and receive the full $2,000 monthly pension without any actuarial reductions for early retirement. In essence, the company's pension plan would be "kicking in" an extra $700 per month for life to John if he elects to retire at age 60 (his pension will not be reduced from $2,000 to $1,300).

Some pension plans offer *partial* early retirement subsidies rather than full subsidies. This means that an employee's pension will be slightly reduced to reflect early retirement, but not to the extent that it would have been reduced if a full actuarial reduction were applied. Therefore, a plan offering a partial early retirement subsidy may provide John with $1,600 per month if he retires early at age 60 (his pension is only reduced by $400 per month). Remember, the reduction on his $2,000 accrued benefit would have been $700 per month to $1,300, if the plan offered no early retirement subsidy.

1.1 How does the early retirement subsidy affect an alternate payee under a QDRO?

Under federal law, an alternate payee under a QDRO may receive a share of the early retirement subsidy granted to the plan participant, but only if the QDRO includes language that gives him or her the subsidy. There is also another important restriction. *An alternate payee can receive a portion of the early retirement subsidy only if the participant retires early and receives the subsidy himself.* In other words, if alternate payees elect to receive their share of the benefits when the participants reach the plan's earliest retirement age, they won't get any early retirement subsidy if the participants decide to keep working. It is important to understand that early retirement subsidies were designed to provide employees with an incentive to retire early. Many companies try to encourage employees to retire early so they can be replaced by younger employees at much lower wages. An early retirement subsidy was not meant to be a bonus to former spouses under QDROs. That is why alternate payees under a QDRO cannot receive a share of the early retirement subsidy until the participants actually retire early and receive a subsidy themselves. In that case, once a participant subsequently retires early, an alternate payee can receive a share of the early retirement subsidy, but only if the QDRO itself contains the necessary language.

See Section 8 in Sample 8. It contains language allowing the alternate payee to begin receiving her share of the pension on or after the participant's earliest retirement age, even if the participant keeps working. Remember, the trigger for the alternate payee starting benefits is based on the age of the employee, not on the age of the alternate payee. If the alternate payee does elect to commence benefits on the earliest possible date while the employee is still working, her share of the benefits will be fully actuarially reduced to reflect her earlier commencement of benefits. She will only receive an *unsubsidized* pension (without any early retirement subsidy). However, Section 8 of the sample QDRO also states that if the participant retires early after the alternate payee has already started her fully reduced pension, then the alternate payee's share shall be "recalculated" to provide her with a pro rata share of the early retirement subsidy received by the participant on the date of his retirement.

1.2 What if a shared payment QDRO is used?

By its very name, a shared payment QDRO means that the alternate payee will simply share in the pension payments made to the participant when he retires. Chapter 3 discusses this approach in detail. As a result, the alternate payee must wait for the participant to actually retire before she can begin receiving her share of the benefits. If you (or your attorney) use a shared payment type of QDRO, it is still appropriate to include "early retirement subsidy" language so that you can share in any subsidies received by the participant if he retires before his normal retirement age.

1.3 When can you receive benefits under a defined contribution plan?

Under most defined benefit pension plans, an alternate payee may generally not start receiving her share of the benefits until the participant himself is eligible for a distribution. However, under most defined contribution plans (such as a 401(k) or profit-sharing plan), companies allow alternate payees to receive their distributions right away, as soon as the QDRO is approved. Again, this is usually the case only for defined contribution plans. Your defined contribution QDRO should therefore include language stating that the alternate payee may commence her share of the benefits "as soon as administratively feasible following the date the QDRO is approved by the plan administrator, or upon the participant's earliest permitted distribution date, if later." In this way, you can get an immediate distribution if the company permits one.

Even though many companies permit immediate distributions for alternate payees under defined contribution plan QDROs, it is not something they are required to do by law. I know of cases where an attorney has promised a client that the client will receive the distribution right away once the QDRO is approved, only to find out later that the company in question does not permit immediate distributions. Therefore, before you rely on information from your attorney, it would be wise to contact the plan administrator to inquire about the date you could first receive your distribution. Don't buy that new house until you get confirmation from the plan, because your intended down payment could be 20 years in the waiting. And do you really want to spend time and money going after your attorney for providing misleading information?

2. Direct Distribution or Rollover to an Individual Retirement Account

When you become eligible to receive your distribution under the defined contribution plan, you can choose from any payment options available under the plan. In most cases, alternate payees choose their benefits in the form of a single lump sum cash payment. If you do choose this form of payment, remember that the plan administrator will automatically withhold 20 percent of the taxable portion of your distribution. This 20 percent withholding is not a penalty. It is simply up-front tax withholding for federal income tax purposes. To avoid this 20 percent withholding, you may instruct the plan administrator to roll over your distribution to an individual retirement account (IRA) that you may set up at a bank. Usually the distribution election form that you fill out at the time of your distribution will provide you with the rollover option. Again, if you want the cash, the plan will automatically withhold 20 percent for federal income tax purposes, so plan your spending wisely.

3. Establishing Separate Accounts

If the plan does not permit you to receive an immediate distribution, the plan administrator is required to segregate your share of the total account balance and establish a separate account in your name. You are then entitled to any interest and investment gains or losses that are attributable to your assigned share of the account balance until the date of distribution. To guarantee that you will receive such investment gains, your QDRO should include this provision. If your QDRO is silent on the issue of interest or investment gains, the plan may provide you with a frozen amount when the time comes. Therefore, if your QDRO was approved in 1985 and it provided you with $20,000, it is theoretically possible that the plan will give you only $20,000, even if your distribution is received in the year 2000. Imagine that. This means that the 15 years of growth on your share of the funds will go to your ex-husband. That's why it's important for your QDRO to include language stating that you are entitled to any interest and investment gains or losses that are attributable to your share of the account balance from the date of divorce to the date that you receive your distribution. Also, many plans will permit alternate payees to direct their own investments under a variety of mutual fund alternatives available under the plan.

CHAPTER 9

Are You Entitled to Receive Your Share of the Pension for Your Entire Lifetime? (If So, How Can You Secure a Lifetime Pension?)

If you were awarded a portion of your ex-husband's pension benefits at divorce as a part of the property settlement, you should be entitled to receive your share of the benefits for your entire lifetime. Unfortunately, this doesn't always happen. Since many attorneys are not familiar with the QDRO process, the QDROs they draft could shortchange you considerably. According to domestic relations courts throughout the country, the nonparticipant spouse is considered a co-owner of the pension benefits earned by the participant during the marriage. I said it before and I'll say it again: you do not merely stand in the shoes of a creditor. You have an equal ownership interest in the marital portion of the pension benefits. But because of the technical requirements of QDROs, former spouses can lose their rights to a lifetime stream of pension income even if they were awarded an equitable share of the pension benefits at divorce.

There are several ways to assure that you will receive your share of the pension benefits for your entire lifetime. It really depends on the type of QDRO that you use. As discussed in Chapter 3, there are two types of QDROs for defined benefit pension plans. One is called a separate interest QDRO, and the other is a shared payment QDRO. You had better know the difference if you want to receive a lifetime of pension benefits.

1. Use of a Separate Interest QDRO

The vast majority of QDROs prepared today use the separate interest approach. Remember, under this approach, the alternate payee receives her share of the benefits for her entire lifetime, once they commence. When you elect to commence benefits, they will be *actuarially adjusted* to your own life expectancy. This is the easiest way to assure a lifetime pension for yourself. And because the pension payments are tied to your life expectancy, your ex-husband does not have to elect a joint and survivor annuity at retirement for your protection.

The QDRO should, however, include "preretirement" survivorship protection for you in case your ex-husband dies before retirement and before you elect to start receiving your share of the benefits.

You also should be aware that if a separate interest QDRO was used in your case, you may be receiving a smaller benefit than you intended if you are younger than your ex-husband. Because the benefits will be tied to your life expectancy, they will be reduced if you are younger than your ex-husband. This is because you have a longer life expectancy. For example, if your QDRO provides you with $1,000 per month from your ex-husband's pension benefits, don't be alarmed if you receive only $700 per month when you elect to start your pension. The plan administrator may have to reduce the $1,000 in order to convert it to your own lifetime. If you are only a couple of years younger than your ex-husband, the reduction will be relatively small. However, if you are significantly younger than him, the reduction to your pension will grow substantially. And when you add this *actuarial reduction* to a further reduction if you elect to start your benefits early before your ex-husband's normal retirement age of 65, you may be shocked to realize that you will be receiving only $400 per month rather than $1,000. So, if you believe the plan administrator made a mistake when you receive that first check in the mail, be sure to ask how it determined the amount payable to you. Ask if the adjustment was due to an early retirement commencement reduction or an actuarial reduction to convert the pension benefits to your own life expectancy.

2. Use of a Shared Payment QDRO

Under the shared payment approach, the alternate payee's share of the benefits is not actuarially adjusted to her own life expectancy. The alternate payee simply shares in a portion of the participant's pension payments commencing when the participant himself retires. This type of QDRO can be more dangerous for you if it does not include adequate survivorship protection. Under a shared payment QDRO, your payments will cease on the death of the participant, unless the QDRO includes both pre-retirement and postretirement joint and survivor protection.

Along with the standard pre-retirement survivor protection that is necessary in each type of QDRO, you must make sure that the QDRO includes a paragraph stating that you (the alternate payee) will be treated as the participant's surviving spouse with respect to the plan's postretirement survivor annuity. This means that when your ex-husband retires, he will be required to elect his benefits in the form of a reduced joint and survivor annuity. Under this form of payment, you will receive a survivor pension for the rest of your life if your ex-husband predeceases you. Again, this form of payment is not automatic. The QDRO must include this postretirement survivor protection language for you. If you don't see it, call your attorney. It can mean the difference between of lifetime of pension income or nothing at all if your ex-husband dies prematurely.

3. Contact the Plan Administrator If Uncertain

Many QDROs are rather vague regarding the distinction between separate interest and shared payment. If you read your QDRO, it may not be clear whether your attorney used the separate interest approach or the shared payment approach. For example, your QDRO may include language stating that you must wait for your ex-husband to retire before you can start your share of the pension benefits. However, your attorney may have intended to use a separate interest approach. As a result, your attorney did not include postretirement survivorship protection for you because this is not necessary under a separate interest QDRO. But the plan administrator may be confused when it interprets the QDRO and treat it as a shared payment QDRO. And because the QDRO doesn't have postretirement survivorship protection, you could be out of luck if your ex-husband predeceases you. You will lose all rights to any continued pension benefits on his death.

When I draft a QDRO for a client, I include language that makes it crystal clear whether I am using a separate interest QDRO or a shared payment QDRO. (See Section 8 in Sample 8.) But the QDRO your attorney drafted for you may not be this clear. Contact the pension administrator once your QDRO is approved to discuss your rights to a lifetime of pension income. Simply ask the administrator which approach it adopted when interpreting and approving your QDRO. If it interpreted your QDRO as a shared payment QDRO, be sure that it includes postretirement survivorship protection for you. If it doesn't, call your attorney right away to get your QDRO amended.

4. What about a Defined Contribution Plan?

You really don't have to worry about receiving a lifetime pension from a defined contribution plan. As you recall, a defined contribution plan, such as a 401(k) plan, contains an account balance for each plan participant. If the QDRO awards you a portion of the total account balance, you can generally receive your share of the benefits in the form of a single lump sum cash payment. Whether or not you can receive it immediately after the approval of the QDRO depends on the particular plan administrator. Once your QDRO is approved, you should ask the plan administrator if you are entitled to immediate payment.

Some defined contribution plans offer distributions in the form of installment payments in addition to the standard lump sum option. You may even be permitted to choose an installment payment for the term of your anticipated life expectancy. But almost everyone elects to take the cash and run.

CHAPTER 10

Is It Too Late to Draft a QDRO Now? (Your Divorce Occurred Years Ago)

If your attorney failed to draft a QDRO when you divorced, it may not be too late to draft one now, if your ex-husband is still alive. Whether your ex-husband is an active employee or a retiree, a QDRO can still be drafted to provide you with a portion of his pension benefits. It also does not matter whether he already quit his job, as long as he has a vested right to a future pension benefit. A vesting schedule generally applies to participants covered under a defined benefit pension plan. It's a way for a company to avoid paying lifetime pension benefits to someone who has worked for the company for only a short time.

There are several types of vesting schedules for pension plans. For example, participants may become fully vested in their accrued benefit when they have been employed for five or more years. This is called *five-year cliff vesting*. It means that if participants quit their job before completing five years of service, they will be 0 percent vested, and thus entitled to no future pension. However, once they reach five years of service, they are considered 100 percent vested in their accrued benefit and will be entitled to a future pension starting at age 65. Remember, those who quit their job with a vested pension right may not be able to start receiving their pension immediately. A terminated participant's pension benefits generally start on an unreduced basis when the participant reaches the plan's "normal retirement age," which is usually age 65.

The first thing you should do is check your original divorce decree or separation agreement to see if you were awarded a portion of your ex-husband's pension benefits. If you were, then get the QDRO done now, without further delay. It is also very important to get the QDRO done before your ex-husband retires. As discussed in Chapter 12, it may be too late for you to get a lifetime pension if he does retire before the QDRO is drafted. This is because he may have chosen a single life pension (without any survivorship benefits) when he retired, and under all pension plans, once a retiree elects a form of payment, it is irrevocable. Your ex-husband may not later change his election to provide any survivorship benefits to anyone. Also, it's too late to draft a separate interest QDRO if the participant has retired. Further, it may be impossible for you to get missed pension payments if your QDRO is delayed beyond your ex-husband's date of retirement.

And, if your ex-husband dies before the QDRO is drafted, you may as well forget about getting any of the pension benefits awarded to you at the divorce. See Chapter 13 for a detailed discussion of the impact of the death of the participant before a QDRO is drafted. You have just two chances to see any pension if this happens — slim and fat.

1. The Importance of Drafting a 401(k) Plan QDRO before Your Ex-Husband Terminates His Employment

If you were awarded a portion of your ex-husband's 401(k) benefits when you divorced, it is even more important to draft the QDRO right away. This is because a participant may become eligible to receive his full account balance under the plan much sooner than you think. When you think about your ex-husband's retirement benefits, you may be thinking of a payment that will start at some point in the distant future, especially if he was only 32 years old when you divorced. But under a defined contribution plan, a participant becomes eligible for a distribution not only upon his retirement, but also upon his earlier termination of employment — something that may not have been anticipated when the divorce occurred.

If you just now discovered that a QDRO was not prepared for you at the time of divorce, you had better hope that your ex-husband is still employed if you were awarded a portion of his 401(k) benefits. If he quit his job, it's very likely that he already took his distribution from the plan. Very few participants choose to maintain their accounts under the plan after they terminate their employment. They usually elect an immediate lump sum distribution. And if your ex-husband did choose to receive his total account balance when he terminated his employment, it is absolutely too late to prepare a QDRO now. Even if you drafted a QDRO and submitted it to the plan administrator, there is nothing the administrator could do about it. No funds remain to pay your share of the account balance. Once the plan administrator made the distribution to your ex-husband, it discharged all of its plan liability with respect to him.

2. What If the Plan Makes a Distribution to Your Ex-Husband While the QDRO Process Is Pending?

Because the people who administer pension plans are only human, they sometimes make mistakes regarding plan distributions. Under federal law, if a plan administrator receives a court order that purports to be a QDRO, it must separately account for the alternate payee's share of the benefits to prevent a distribution from being made to the participant. I have witnessed many inadvertent and premature distributions by plan administrators over the years when a QDRO was pending. For example, perhaps your attorney drafted a QDRO for you when you divorced that awarded you 50 percent of the total account balance under your ex-husband's 401(k) plan. What if the QDRO was faulty and the plan administrator rejected your attorney's draft QDRO? Once your divorce is finalized, you and your attorney may lose track of each other. Further, because the attorney's "billable" hours are no longer accumulating in your case, he or she may be very reluctant to spend any more time representing you after the divorce is over. In other words, your attorney might forget to tie up some loose ends. And the mother of all loose ends is a QDRO in limbo (one that has not yet been approved by the plan administrator). Your attorney may think the case is closed, but a major time bomb is ticking in his or her files.

3. Is There an 18-Month Maximum Segregation Period for Pending QDROs?

There is often some confusion about the plan administrator's time limitation for determining whether a domestic relations order qualifies as a QDRO under Section 414(p) of the Internal Revenue Code. A common misconception is that the plan administrator has 18 months to determine the qualified status of an order. This is not true. An 18-month period does come into play, however, when benefits to be paid to the alternate payee under a domestic relations order are postponed and separately accounted for during the period in which a plan administrator is determining whether the order qualifies as a QDRO.

Under federal law, a plan administrator must separately account for any amounts that would have been paid to an alternate payee if the order had been determined to be a QDRO. If this order is not determined to be a qualified domestic relations order within 18 months after the date on which the first payment would have otherwise been made to the alternate payee, then these *segregated* amounts (amounts that were separately accounted for, including any interest on them) must be paid by the plan administrator to the person or persons entitled to them as if there had been no domestic relations order (that is, to the plan participant or his or her beneficiaries). If the court order (or an amended court order) is determined to be a QDRO within this 18-month period, the segregated amounts called for under the order will be distributed to the alternate payee in line with the terms of the QDRO.

The application of this 18-month period should not be confused with the plan administrator's requirement to determine the qualified status of the order within a reasonable period of time after receiving it. Under federal law, plan administrators must make their determinations about the qualified status of court orders within a "reasonable period of time" after receiving the order. Unfortunately, the term "reasonable" is not defined anywhere in the law. This has the result that many companies take many, many months to review QDROs. While this delay might make sense in a company like General Motors, certainly a small company should review a QDRO within days or a couple of weeks. After all, it may only be one of several QDROs received by them in the whole year.

It is therefore in the best interests of the plan administrator to begin reviewing domestic relations orders as soon as they are submitted.

This is especially true when plan participants are already receiving their pension benefits. Prompt action should be taken to segregate funds and separately account for the amounts identified as payable to the alternate payee. In all likelihood, the "reasonable period" test will be a facts-and-circumstances determination if it ever is challenged. Plan administrators must be prepared to show that they refrained from any undue or deliberate delay during the determination period, particularly in cases where benefits are immediately payable to the alternate payee.

4. Check for a Possible Rollover to an Individual Retirement Account

If you do discover the worst — that your ex-husband has already taken his distribution from the 401(k) plan — it may not be too late for you to realize your fair share of the benefits. Obviously, it's too late to draft a QDRO, because there are no remaining funds in the plan. However, many plan participants, your ex-husband included, may have chosen to roll over his distribution to an individual retirement account (IRA) to avoid an immediate taxation of his benefits. Your first response should be to contact an attorney who should be able to easily determine whether your ex-husband transferred his 401(k) assets to an IRA. If so, your attorney can reopen your case and you should be able to recover your share of the account balance. A court order could direct the IRA administrator to segregate the funds into two separate accounts, one of which is in your name.

If your ex-husband chose to receive a cash distribution rather than roll it over into an IRA, it may be more difficult for you to obtain your rightful share of the benefits, especially if he has already spent your share. Your attorney should be able to help you with this scenario as well, but it could be more costly to you and is less likely to succeed.

5. What If the Original Divorce Decree Was Silent on the Pension Issue?

The QDRO laws came into existence in late 1984. As a result, if your divorce or dissolution occurred in 1985 or later, your attorney should have addressed the pension issue if your ex-husband was covered by a pension or savings plan at any time during your marriage. Obviously, in the early era of QDROs (1985–89), a divorce attorney would have been more likely to forget about the pension issue when dividing up the assets of the parties. In the 1990s, however, most divorce attorneys became familiar with the QDRO laws, although perhaps not familiar enough to draft them properly.

Unfortunately, once a divorce is finalized, it is often extremely difficult to reopen the case later. If you were not awarded a portion of your ex-husband's pension benefits in your original property settlement or separation agreement, courts are very leery about upsetting the applecart years later. But you shouldn't give up if you notice that your 1992 divorce decree was silent on the pension issue and you are sure that your ex-husband participated in a pension plan during the years of your marriage. You should definitely contact an attorney now to discuss this issue. Whether your new attorney tries to reopen the case to redistribute the original property settlement or considers a malpractice case against your divorce attorney, it is in your best interests not to give up. Although I am not an advocate of malpractice suits, forgetting about a significant asset like the pension is a terrible blunder on your attorney's part, and if there ever was a good reason for a malpractice suit, this is one of them.

Some US jurisdictions make it easy to reopen an old divorce case if the pension issue was totally left off the table at the time of divorce. Courts recognize that a pension benefit may be the parties' largest marital asset. They also realize that most divorce attorneys are unfamiliar with QDROs. For these two reasons, the court may treat your original property settlement as incomplete and allow the parties to go back to court to equitably divide your ex-husband's pension benefits.

6. The Buildup of Child Support or Alimony Arrearage after Divorce

You may have already been awarded a portion of your ex-husband's pension benefits at divorce. Perhaps the QDRO was already prepared for you and approved by the plan administrator. So, as far as your "property" interests in the pension are concerned, it's a done deal: someday, you will start receiving your share of the pension benefits. But what if your ex-husband is delinquent in making your child support or alimony payments? Even if your divorce was years ago, it should still be possible to obtain a QDRO today solely to catch up on your child support or alimony arrearage. It does not matter if you already have a QDRO in place giving you your property rights to the pension. That is a separate issue. It is perfectly acceptable to prepare a second QDRO today to recoup past-due child support or alimony payments from the "remainder" of your ex-husband's share of the pension or savings plan benefits. The portion of the pension not awarded to you at the time of your divorce (for your property rights) could be attached via a new QDRO today for child support or alimony purposes. There is no limit to the amount of your ex-husband's benefits that you could receive via a QDRO. Under the QDRO provisions of the law, an alternate payee could receive up to 100 percent of the participant's pension or savings plan benefits.

Let's look at an example. Assume that Jane was divorced from Tom in 1995 and was awarded 50 percent of the total account balance in Tom's 401(k) plan. Because his total account balance was $50,000 when they divorced, a QDRO was prepared that provided Jane with $25,000 as of June 1, 1995, their date of divorce. Of course, Tom was free to keep the remaining $25,000. Let's assume that Jane has already received her $25,000 from the first QDRO. Now let's zoom forward to November 1, 2002. On this date, Tom is delinquent in his child support payments, with a total arrearage of $8,000. Jane's first QDRO gave her half of Tom's total account balance as *her own separate property right*, but now Jane can prepare a new QDRO in order to recoup the child support arrearage. A new QDRO can now be prepared that will provide Jane with $8,000 in child support arrearage; and in all likelihood, she could receive her distribution immediately after the plan administrator approves the QDRO.

Don't forget about this very important use for QDROs. Chapter 11 discusses QDROs for child support and alimony in further detail. It also contains sample QDROs to use in obtaining past-due child support and alimony.

CHAPTER 11

What about Past-Due
Child Support and Alimony
(Can You Use a QDRO for This?)

You can use a QDRO to obtain past-due child support or alimony payments. This is one of the reasons why QDROs were created by Congress in 1984 — for the express purpose of obtaining child support and alimony payments.

1. Does This Sound Familiar?

Before going into the details of how to use a QDRO to obtain past-due child support or alimony, does this story sound familiar? When Susan H. divorced, her ex-husband was required to send her $600 per month in child support for her three boys. In the first several months after the divorce, she received her payments like clockwork. On the 15th of every month, she ran out to the mailbox and grabbed her new subscription to *Women's Sports & Fitness* and her child support check. Then, in the fourth month after the divorce, something unusual happened. Susan didn't receive her monthly child support payment. Because it was close to Christmas, she assumed the check had been delayed in the mail. Well, by July of the next year, she started wondering where that December payment was. Not to mention January, February,

March, April, May, and June. Could it be? Could the father of "Daddy's little boys" have stopped sending the monthly support checks?

So in July, Susan H. contacted the child support enforcement agency for their help. Not much we can do, they told her. It's very difficult to go after your ex-husband, they said, because he moved to Mars, Alabama, while you're still living here in Venus, Ohio. So Susan H. hired an attorney. She was determined to see justice done, not to mention that she was desperate for the money. Meanwhile, two months and $4,000 later, Mr. H. was finally served with legal papers and appeared in front of Judge Stone in the Venus County Court of Common Pleas-Domestic Relations Division. He was given a choice: either reinstate the $600 per month child support payments, or spend some time in jail. He opted for the child support payments. And then, like magic, on the 15th day of the following month, Susan was shocked to see a child support payment in the mailbox hiding under her new subscription to *Death By Chocolate: From French Pastries to Fondue*. She won. Justice had prevailed. However, on the 15th of the following month, there was no check in the mailbox — and it wasn't even near Christmas. What's a mother to do now? It cost Susan more than $4,000 in legal fees to get that $600 check. Now what? Should she get another attorney and spend another $4,000 in the hopes of getting another $600 check? Susan is certainly not alone. There are literally millions of deadbeat dads across the US.

Susan's attorney overlooked the fact that Mr. H. was a participant in Acme Tool & Die's 401(k) plan. His account balance was more than $20,000. Had the attorney prepared a QDRO and submitted it to Acme Tool & Die, Susan could have received all of her child support arrearage in one lump sum payment immediately — no muss, no fuss — no court hearings, no subpoenas, no threat of jail time for the ex-husband — although this would have been a bonus from her perspective. And subsequent QDROs could be sent in the future if Mr. H. failed to send his continuing support payments in a timely fashion.

2. QDROs for Child Support and Alimony

One of the most overlooked areas of QDROs is in the area of child support and alimony. Very few attorneys (and very few women in the United States) know about this very important use for QDROs. With the deadbeat dad population growing by leaps and bounds everyday, a QDRO should now be considered your first line of defense in obtaining these overdue assets. Millions of women throughout the country are owed past-due child support or alimony (also known as spousal support).

A majority of American workers are covered under some sort of pension plan nowadays. Many are covered under a defined contribution plan, such as a 401(k) plan or profit-sharing plan. If your ex-husband is covered under a pension or 401(k) plan, there may be a green light at the end of the tunnel for you. And it's not the lights from an oncoming train, *it's cash*, and it could be yours. Assume your ex-husband has built up an arrearage in alimony of $5,000, for example. You can submit a QDRO to the plan administrator of the company where he is employed, for the sole purpose of providing you with the $5,000 arrearage. And here's the beauty. Even though your ex-husband is not currently eligible to receive a distribution under the plan until he retires or terminates his employment, most companies will provide the alternate payee under a defined contribution plan QDRO with an immediate distribution, once the QDRO has been approved. You can get your $5,000 immediately. You do not have to wait for your ex-husband to retire.

3. Using Multiple QDROs

In the game of Monopoly, there is no limit to the number of times that you can "pass Go and collect $200." The same goes for QDROs. There is no limit to the number of QDROs that you can submit to a company from time to time, especially if they are for past-due child support or alimony purposes. Let's assume that you have just sent a QDRO to your ex-husband's company to receive $5,000 in past-due child support payments. In three weeks, you receive the $5,000. Now let's assume that another year passes and your ex-husband, the deadbeat that he is, builds up another $2,000 in child support arrearage. You have every right to go ahead and submit a second QDRO to the plan administrator requesting payment of the new $2,000 arrearage. Although you should avoid sending a new QDRO to the company every month in which your ex-husband is delinquent in his support obligation (the judge might not take kindly to signing a QDRO for you every month), you can certainly take advantage of a new QDRO every year or so.

4. A Tax Tip for Child Support QDROs

For a QDRO to be approved by the plan administrator, it must include the name of the alternate payee (the individual who is to receive a portion of the participant's benefits). An alternate payee can be either the spouse, the former spouse, or the dependent child of the participant. When an attorney drafts a QDRO, whether it's for property right, alimony, or child support purposes, he or she will generally, by default, name the former spouse as the alternate payee. In other words, if you ask your attorney to draft a QDRO so that you can receive past-due child support payments from your ex-husband, he or she will probably list you as the "alternate payee" under the QDRO. Under federal law, whenever a QDRO is administered by a company and the former spouse is named as the alternate payee, the alternate payee will be taxed on the money received. Therefore, if your QDRO names you as the alternate payee, even if it is for child support purposes, you will be responsible for any taxes due on the distribution that you receive from your ex-husband's 401(k) plan.

Here's a tip that could save you a lot of money. If your QDRO is for child support purposes, your attorney may want to consider listing your child as the alternate payee in the QDRO itself, rather than identifying you as the alternate payee. A company will accept the QDRO either way, but if the child is named as the alternate payee, then your ex-husband will be taxed on the amount of money you receive from the plan. However, if your attorney lists you as the alternate payee, you will be taxed on this money. After all, if your ex-husband had made timely child support payments each month, he would have the legal responsibility of paying taxes on the amounts paid to you. This is because child support payments are not considered a deductible expense for him by the Internal Revenue Service. So why should he be able to "duck" or shift the tax burden to you, simply because you were forced into submitting a QDRO to get past-due child support payments as a result of his delinquency in payments?

So, if you ask an attorney to prepare a child support QDRO for you, be sure to give him or her this tax tip. My guess is that he or she is not aware of this rather obscure but important provision. Alternatively, if you use one of the sample QDROs in this book, you may want to list your child(ren) as the alternate payee(s) in the QDRO rather than listing yourself, if it is for child support arrearage purposes. Beware, however. If your child is no longer a minor and you do not have a good relationship with him or her any longer, you may want to name yourself as the alternate payee rather than your child. After all, wouldn't you rather pay taxes on your QDRO distribution, rather than having that distribution go to an adult child that you haven't seen in ten years?

5. Getting Past-Due Child Support Payments or Alimony from a Defined Contribution Plan

Because defined contribution plans consist of individual employee accounts (individual pots of money) that grow each year as a result of the employee's contributions, plan contributions, and investment earnings, these are the ideal plans for obtaining past-due child support or alimony. A QDRO can be prepared that will require your ex-husband's company to distribute the entire arrearage to you in a single, lump sum payment. Remember that a QDRO can only provide up to 100 percent of the participant's total vested account balance at any point in time. The term *vested* refers to the portion of his account which he has already *earned* and is considered nonforfeitable. For example, many 401(k) plans include a vesting schedule in which the participant's vesting status grows by 20 percent per year. In his first year of plan participation, he is 20 percent vested in his total account balance. This means that if he were to quit at this time, he would be entitled to receive only 20 percent of his total account balance. The remainder would revert to the plan. Once a participant is 100 percent vested, he is eligible to receive all of the funds in his account when he terminates his employment or retires. Usually, vesting schedules apply only to plan contributions made by the employer. A participant is always 100 percent vested in his own employee contributions. You can think of vesting as that portion of the participant's benefits that he would be entitled to if he were to immediately quit his employment or retire.

Also, many plan administrators will make immediate distributions to an alternate payee once the QDRO is approved. This is especially true for defined contribution plans. Even though your ex-husband may not yet be entitled to a plan distribution because he is still working, the company will send you the full child support or alimony arrearage as called for under the terms of the QDRO, once it is approved by the plan administrator. From the company's perspective, it would rather "cash you out" instead of maintaining separate accounts in your name for 10 or 20 years. (See the sample QDROs at the end of this chapter for use in drafting a child support QDRO for a defined contribution plan.)

6. Getting Past-Due Child Support Payments or Alimony from a Defined Benefit Pension Plan

If your ex-husband is covered only under a defined benefit pension plan, which will pay him a monthly pension check for life when he retires, it is more difficult to obtain past-due child support or alimony right away using a QDRO. Remember, in a defined benefit pension plan, individual accounts are not established for any plan participants. As a result, there is no "pot of money" from which to take your child support arrearage. This does not mean that you are necessarily out of luck. You may still draft a QDRO that provides you with a portion of your ex-husband's monthly pension benefit once he becomes eligible for early retirement. Then, even if he does not retire when he is first eligible to do so under the plan, you could start to receive your share of the benefits at that time. However, because defined benefit pension plans do not typically provide for lump sum distributions, you may not be able to receive your child support or alimony arrearage in the form of an immediate lump sum payment. But your arrearage payments can be received on a monthly basis for a specified period of time. The amount of each monthly payment, however, cannot exceed your ex-husband's total accrued benefit under the plan.

For example, let's assume that your ex-husband has already accrued a benefit of $500 per month under his defined benefit pension plan. Let's also assume that he is currently 55 years old and has already satisfied the plan's early retirement eligibility provisions: he could retire now if he wanted to. Many pension plans include early retirement provisions to encourage employees to retire before their 65th birthday. You can prepare and submit a QDRO that would pay you a monthly portion of your ex-husband's accrued benefit, starting immediately. This is true even if he continues working beyond his early retirement eligibility date. If your alimony arrearage is $3,000, for example, you could include language in the QDRO that would provide you with $300 per month payable for 10 months. (See Sample 1 and Sample 2 for use in drafting QDROs for a child support arrearage. You'll notice that the child support QDRO for the defined benefit plans does not include any survivor protection language. Survivor language is intended to provide alternate payees with lifetime incomes upon the death of the participant. Because child support QDROs are intended to provide only a finite amount based on the arrearage, a judge will not likely sign a QDRO that attempts to give lifetime survivor benefits.

SAMPLE 1
TO OBTAIN PAST-DUE CHILD SUPPORT
(From a defined benefit pension plan)

IN THE COURT OF COMMON PLEAS
DIVISION OF DOMESTIC RELATIONS

(*Enter Caption Here*)   )
)   CASE NO. (*Enter Case*)
)
)   JUDGE (*Enter Judge*)
)
)   QUALIFIED DOMESTIC
)   RELATIONS ORDER

IT IS HEREBY ORDERED AS FOLLOWS:

1. Effect of this Order as a Qualified Domestic Relations Order: This Order creates and recognizes the existence of an Alternate Payee's right to receive a portion of the Participant's benefits payable under an employer sponsored defined benefit pension plan that is qualified under Section 401 of the Internal Revenue Code (the "Code") and the Employee Retirement Income Security Act of 1974 ("ERISA"). It is intended to constitute a Qualified Domestic Relations Order ("QDRO") under Section 414(p) of the Code and Section 206(d)(3) of ERISA.

2. Participant Information: The name, last known address, social security number, and date of birth of the plan "Participant" is:

Name: _____

Address: _____

Social Security Number: _____

Date of Birth: _____

3. Alternate Payee Information: The name, last known address, social security number, and date of birth of the "Alternate Payee" is:

Name: _____

Address: _____

Social Security Number: _____

Date of Birth: _____

The Alternate Payee shall have the duty to notify the Plan Administrator in writing of any changes in her or his mailing address subsequent to the entry of this Order.

4. Plan Name: The name of the Plan to which this Order applies is the_____ (hereinafter referred to as the "Plan"). Further, any successor plan to the Plan or any other plan(s), to which liability for provision of the Participant's benefits described below is incurred, shall also be subject to the terms of this Order. Also, any benefits accrued by the Participant under a predecessor plan of the employer or any other defined benefit plan sponsored by the Participant's employer, where liability for benefits accrued under such predecessor plan or other defined benefit plan has been transferred to the Plan, shall also be subject to the terms of this Order.

Any changes in Plan Administrator, Plan Sponsor, or name of the Plan shall not affect the Alternate Payee's rights as stipulated under this Order.

5. Pursuant to State Domestic Relations Law: This Order is entered pursuant to the authority granted in the applicable domestic relations laws of the State of _____.

6. For Provision of Marital Property Rights: This Order relates to the provision of past-due "child support" to the Alternate Payee as a result of the Order of Divorce between the Participant and the Alternate Payee.

7. Amount of Alternate Payee's Benefit: From the pension benefits otherwise payable to the Participant each month, this Order assigns to the Alternate Payee an amount equal to **Fifty Percent (50%)** of each such monthly pension payment, commencing upon the Participant's date of retirement. The Alternate Payee shall continue to receive her or his assigned share of the monthly benefits until such time as she or he has received a total of $ _____from the Plan (or until the earlier to occur of her or his death or the Participant's death).

8. Death of Alternate Payee: If the Alternate Payee predeceases the Participant, her or his share of the benefits shall revert to the Participant.

9. Savings Clause: This Order is not intended to, and shall not be construed in such a manner as to, require the Plan:

    (a)   to provide any type or form of benefit option not otherwise provided under the terms of the Plan;

    (b)   to require the Plan to provide increased benefits determined on the basis of actuarial value; or

    (c)   to require the payment of any benefits to the alternate Payee that are required to be paid to another alternate payee under another order that was previously deemed to be a QDRO.

10. Constructive Receipt: In the event that the Plan Trustee inadvertently pays to the Participant any benefits that are assigned to the Alternate Payee pursuant to the terms of this Order, the Participant shall immediately reimburse the Alternate Payee to the extent that he or she has received such benefit payments, and shall forthwith pay such amounts so received directly to the Alternate Payee within ten (10) days of receipt.

11. Continued Jurisdiction: The Court shall retain jurisdiction with respect to this Order to the extent required to maintain its qualified status and the original intent of the parties as stipulated herein. The Court shall also retain jurisdiction to enter such further orders as are necessary to enforce the assignment of benefits to the Alternate Payee as set forth herein.

12. Plan Termination: If the Plan is terminated, whether on a voluntary or involuntary basis, and the Participant's benefits become guaranteed by the Pension Benefit Guaranty Corporation ("PBGC"), the Alternate Payee's benefits, as stipulated herein, shall also be guaranteed to the same extent in accordance with the Plan's termination rules and in the same ratio as the Participant's benefits are guaranteed by the PBGC.

13. Actions by Participant: The Participant shall not take any actions, affirmative or otherwise, that can circumvent the terms and provisions of this Qualified Domestic Relations Order, or that could diminish or extinguish the rights and entitlements of the Alternate Payee as set forth herein. Should the Participant take any action or inaction to the detriment of the Alternate Payee, he or she shall be required to make sufficient payments **directly** to the Alternate Payee to the extent necessary to neutralize the effects of his or her actions or inactions and to the extent of the Alternate Payee's full entitlements hereunder.

14. Notice of Pending Retirement: Pursuant to the terms of Section 7 above, the Alternate Payee shall commence her or his share of the benefits upon the Participant's actual date of benefit commencement. Therefore, the Participant shall be required to notify the Alternate Payee, in writing, within thirty (30) days prior to his or her actual date of retirement. Such notice shall indicate his or her intentions to retire and his or her elected benefit commencement date. The notice shall be sent via regular, first class mail.

IT IS SO ORDERED.

_____
JUDGE (*Enter Judge*)

SAMPLE 2
TO OBTAIN PAST-DUE CHILD SUPPORT
(From a defined contribution plan, such as a 401(k))

IN THE COURT OF COMMON PLEAS
DIVISION OF DOMESTIC RELATIONS
(Enter County and State Here)

(Enter Caption Here)   )
)   CASE NO. *(Enter Case)*
)
)   JUDGE *(Enter Judge)*
)
)   QUALIFIED DOMESTIC
)   RELATIONS ORDER

IT IS HEREBY ORDERED AS FOLLOWS:

1. Effect of this Order as a Qualified Domestic Relations Order: This Order creates and recognizes the existence of an Alternate Payee's right to receive a portion of the Participant's benefits payable under an employer sponsored defined contribution plan that is qualified under Section 401 of the Internal Revenue Code (the "Code") and the Employee Retirement Income Security Act of 1974 ("ERISA"). It is intended to constitute a Qualified Domestic Relations Order ("QDRO") under Section 414(p) of the Code and Section 206(d)(3) of ERISA.

2. Participant Information: The name, last known address, social security number, and date of birth of the plan "Participant" is:

Name: _____

Address: _____

Social Security Number: _____

Date of Birth: _____

3. Alternate Payee Information: The name, last known address, social security number, and date of birth of the "Alternate Payee" is:

Name: _____

Address: _____

Social Security Number: _____

Date of Birth: _____

SAMPLE 2 — Continued

The Alternate Payee shall have the duty to notify the Plan Administrator in writing of any changes in her or his mailing address subsequent to the entry of this Order.

4. Plan Name: The name of the Plan to which this Order applies is the _____ (hereinafter collectively referred to as the "Plan").

Any changes in Plan Administrator, Plan Sponsor, or name of the Plan shall not affect the Alternate Payee's rights as stipulated under this Order.

5. Pursuant to State Domestic Relations Law: This Order is entered pursuant to the authority granted in the applicable domestic relations laws of the State of _____.

6. For Provision of Past-Due Child Support Payments: This Order relates to the provision of past-due "child support" to the Alternate Payee as a result of the Order of Divorce between the Participant and the Alternate Payee. The total amount of child support arrearage equals $ _____. Therefore, this Order assigns to the Alternate Payee an amount equal to the lesser of **One Hundred Percent (100%)** of the Participant's total vested account balance under the Plan as of **[current date]**, or $ _____.

Additionally, the Alternate Payee shall be entitled to any interest and investment earnings or losses attributable to her or his assigned share of the benefits for periods subsequent to **[current date]**, until the date of total distribution. The Alternate Payee's share of the benefits will be allocated on a pro rata basis among all of the Participant's accounts maintained on his or her behalf under the Plan.

7. Commencement Date and Form of Payment to Alternate Payee: The Alternate Payee shall receive her or his share of the benefits as soon as administratively feasible following the date this Order is approved as a QDRO by the Plan Administrator, or at the earliest date permitted under the Plan or Section 414(p) of the Internal Revenue Code, if later. Benefits will be payable to the Alternate Payee in the form of a single lump sum cash payment.

8. Alternate Payee's Rights and Privileges: On and after the date that this Order is deemed to be a Qualified Domestic Relations Order, but before the Alternate Payee receives her or his total distribution under the Plan, the Alternate Payee shall be entitled to all of the rights and election privileges that are afforded to Plan beneficiaries, including, but not limited to, the rules regarding the right to designate a beneficiary for death benefit purposes.

9. Death of Alternate Payee: In the event of the Alternate Payee's death prior to the Alternate Payee receiving the full amount of benefits called for under this Order, the Alternate Payee's beneficiary, as designated on the appropriate form provided by the Plan Administrator (or in the absence of a beneficiary designation, her or his estate), shall receive the remainder of any unpaid benefits under the terms of this Order.

10. Death of Participant: If the Participant dies **before** the Alternate Payee receives her or his distribution in accordance with the terms of this QDRO, or before the establishment of separate account(s) in the name of the Alternate Payee, such Alternate Payee shall be treated as the surviving spouse of the Participant for any death benefits payable under the Plan to the extent of the full amount of her or his benefits as called for under Paragraph 6 of this Order. Should the Participant predecease the Alternate Payee **after** the new account(s) have been established on her or his behalf, the Participant's death shall in no way affect the Alternate Payee's right to the portion of her or his benefits as stipulated herein.

11. Savings Clause: This Order is not intended to, and shall not be construed in such a manner as to, require the Plan:

(a) to provide any type or form of benefit option not otherwise provided under the terms of the Plan;

(b) to require the Plan to provide increased benefits determined on the basis of actuarial value; or

(c) to require the payment of any benefits to the Alternate Payee that are required to be paid to another alternate payee under another order that was previously deemed to be a QDRO.

12. Tax Treatment of Distributions Made under This Order: For purposes of Sections 402(a)(1) and 72 of the Internal Revenue Code, any Alternate Payee who is the spouse or former spouse of the Participant shall be treated as the distributee of any distribution or payments made to the Alternate Payee under the terms of this Order and, as such, will be required to pay the appropriate federal income taxes on such distribution.

13. Constructive Receipt: In the event that the Plan Trustee inadvertently pays to the Participant any benefits which are assigned to the Alternate Payee pursuant to the terms of this Order, the Participant shall immediately reimburse the Alternate Payee to the extent that he or she has received such benefit payments, and shall forthwith pay such amounts so received directly to the Alternate Payee within ten (10) days of receipt.

14. Continued Jurisdiction: The Court shall retain jurisdiction with respect to this Order to the extent required to maintain its qualified status and the original intent of the parties as stipulated herein. The Court shall also retain jurisdiction to enter such further orders as are necessary to enforce the assignment of benefits to the Alternate Payee as set forth herein.

15. Plan Termination: If the Plan is terminated, the Alternate Payee shall be entitled to receive her or his portion of Participant's benefits as stipulated herein in accordance with the Plan's termination provisions for participants and beneficiaries.

16. Actions By Participant: The Participant shall not take any actions, affirmative or otherwise, that can circumvent the terms and provisions of this Qualified Domestic Relations Order, or that could diminish or extinguish the rights and entitlements of the Alternate Payee as set forth herein. Should the Participant take any action or inaction to the detriment of the Alternate Payee, he or she shall be required to make sufficient payments **directly** to the Alternate Payee to the extent necessary to neutralize the effects of his or her actions or inactions and to the extent of the Alternate Payee's full entitlements hereunder.

IT IS SO ORDERED.

_____
JUDGE (*Enter Judge*)

—————————————— ♂♀ ——————————————

CHAPTER 12

Your Ex-Husband Has Already Retired (Is It Too Late to Draft a QDRO?)

If your attorney forgot to draft a QDRO for you when you divorced and you just found out that your ex-husband has already retired, it is not too late to draft a QDRO. You can draft a QDRO now and submit it to the plan administrator so that you can receive a portion of your ex-husband's pension benefits. Of course, your divorce decree should already have granted you a portion of your ex-husband's pension benefits. If it did not, the judge will probably not sign a QDRO for you now.

1. You Must Use a Shared Payment QDRO If Your Ex-Husband Is Retired

Because your ex-husband is already retired and receiving a monthly pension, it is too late to prepare a separate interest QDRO. (See Chapter 3 for a discussion of the two types of QDROs for defined benefit pension plans.) As you recall, a separate interest QDRO provides the alternate payee with an *actuarially adjusted* separate lifetime pension. Once a participant retires, a plan administrator will generally only accept a shared payment QDRO. Under a shared payment QDRO, you simply share in a portion of each monthly pension check. You can receive your share of the pension only so long as your ex-husband is alive and receiving a pension. Upon his death, your share of the pension will also cease, unless (1) your ex-husband chose a postretirement joint and survivor annuity when he retired; and (2) the QDRO includes language that treats you as a surviving spouse for the postretirement survivor annuity. In more than one case, however, the court held that it was too late to provide an alternate payee with survivor benefits because the husband had remarried and elected his new spouse under a joint and survivor annuity when he retired. Therefore, there is no guarantee that you'll receive a lifetime income if you draft a QDRO after you ex's retirement.

If you are not sure whether your ex-husband chose to receive his benefits in the form of a joint and survivor annuity when he retired, your attorney can obtain this information for you either through a release signed by your ex-husband or by using a subpoena. Alternatively, you can play it safe by simply including postretirement survivorship protection language in the QDRO even if you are not sure. The worst case is that the plan will reject your first draft of the QDRO, which will alert you to the fact that your ex-husband did not elect a survivor form of pension when he retired.

2. A Possible "Catch-22" Situation That Will Destroy Any Chance You Have to Receive a Lifetime Pension

If you don't draft the QDRO before your ex-husband retires, it is possible that you could forfeit a lifetime worth of pension benefits if he dies. You can be caught in the following catch-22 situation. On the one hand, because your ex-husband has already retired, it is too late to prepare a separate interest QDRO, which would have provided you with your own separate lifetime pension. And on the other hand, it is also possible that when your ex-husband retired, he chose to receive his benefits in the form of a single life annuity. This means that he will receive his pension benefits only for as long as he is alive and that upon his death, there will be no survivor benefits payable to anybody. Even if your QDRO includes postretirement survivorship protection for you, it means nothing if your ex-husband had already elected a single life annuity when he retired. No QDRO in the world will pay you a pension benefit after he dies.

This is why it's extremely important for you (or your attorney) to prepare the QDRO at the time of the divorce and get it qualified with the plan administrator immediately thereafter. Otherwise, if your ex-husband retires before the QDRO is drafted, it may be too late to provide you with a lifetime pension. Your only option at that time would be a malpractice suit against your attorney for failing to draft a QDRO when it was needed.

Sample 10 is intended for participants who are already retired and receiving their pension benefits. Pay special attention to Section 7 of the QDRO, which provides how much you are to receive while your ex-husband is alive and receiving benefits. Remember, the start date that you provide must be on a prospective basis (starting at some point in the future — for example, the next month).

3. No Retroactive Pension Payments Are Allowed If Your Ex-Husband Is Already Retired

If your ex-husband retired two years ago and you are now submitting the QDRO for the first time, you can only include language in the QDRO that provides you with payments on a *prospective* basis. This means that you can only get your share of the pension *going forward*. The pension plan administrator will not pay you any amounts that were owed to you for the last two years (if your QDRO had been done when it should have been). Although it's true that you would have been receiving your share of the benefits for the last two years if your attorney had drafted the QDRO when you divorced, a QDRO drafted today cannot instruct the plan administrator to make such retroactive pension payments. I see attorneys make this mistake all the time. They will attempt to prepare a QDRO today that includes the following sentence: "Please pay the alternate payee $200 per month, starting when he retired two years ago." The plan administrator will reject this QDRO. It will only accept language stating that your share of the pension is to start on a prospective basis: "next month," for example. Alternatively, you can include language stating that your share of the benefits is to begin "as soon as administratively feasible following the date the QDRO is approved by the plan administrator."

4. There May Be a Way to Recoup Lost Pension Payments

If your ex-husband did retire years ago, it may still be possible to recoup some of your lost pension payments as if the QDRO had been done on a timely basis. For example, let's assume that your ex-husband retired two years ago with a pension of $800 per month for life, but that you are now preparing a QDRO for the first time. Let's also assume that your monthly share of the pension is $200 (as stated in your divorce decree). In other words, had your attorney drafted the QDRO when you divorced, you would have already been receiving $200 per month for the last two years. Well, it is certainly permissible to draft a QDRO today that provides you with $200 per month, starting with his next pension check, "plus an additional $100 for the next 48 months" (in order to recoup your lost $4,800 in pension payments that you would have received during the first two years of his retirement). In other words, it is perfectly acceptable to include language in a QDRO that pays you back your lost pension payments on a prospective basis. Therefore, rather than getting $200 per month, you will receive $300 per month for the next 48 months and then $200 per month thereafter. In this manner, you will have recouped the payments that you missed before the QDRO was drafted. In the above example, I used a recoupment of an additional $100 per month for 48 months. You could just as easily include a different amount over a different recoupment period (perhaps an additional $200 per month for 24 months; this would pay you $400 for 24 months and then $200 per month thereafter).

You should not make the recoupment period too short. The judge may not permit you to receive too much in the way of additional benefits, because it would make too much of a dent in the participant's total monthly pension. In other words, the judge would not likely let you receive 100 percent of your ex-husband's monthly pension, even if the recoupment period was relatively short.

⚲♀

CHAPTER 13

Your Ex-Husband Has Died
(Is It Too Late to Draft a QDRO?)

This could be your worst nightmare: You were awarded a portion of your ex-husband's pension benefits when you divorced and your attorney never prepared a QDRO. You now find out that your ex-husband has died. The odds are good that you will never see any of the pension benefits that were awarded to you during the divorce. This situation is one of the primary reasons why I decided to write this book — to alert former spouses of the critical need for a QDRO. I cannot emphasize this fact enough. I know of many cases where a former spouse is waiting for a pension check to arrive that will never arrive. Here's an unfortunate scenario.

When the divorce decree awarded Krystal $10,000 from the parties' joint bank account, it became hers instantly upon the signing of the divorce decree. When the decree awarded her the living room furniture, it was hers immediately. The patio furniture? Ditto, it's hers and no one could take it away from her. The pension? Well, the decree awarded Krystal 50 percent of her ex-husband's pension benefits. It was written in black and white, right there in her divorce decree. But wait. It's not hers just yet. The pension is a rare breed. It's one of the only assets that can be awarded during a divorce that does not become the property of the nonparticipant spouse upon the signing of the divorce decree. Imagine that. The divorce court says it's hers. The decree says it's hers. But Congress gave plan administrators the right to say that it's not hers until a QDRO is prepared, submitted to the company, and approved by the pension administrator. And all of this has to be accomplished before Krystal's ex-husband dies. If he dies before the QDRO is prepared and approved, the language awarding her the pension in the divorce decree means nothing.

1. Get the QDRO Done before Your Ex-Husband Dies

With all of the divorce attorneys throughout the country, it's hard to believe that so many QDROs still fall through the cracks. There is only one solution. Spouses who are awarded a portion of the pension benefits must start to take matters into their own hands. You should force the issue with your attorney. Have him or her do the QDRO, or keep calling attorneys until you find one who knows how to get the QDRO done. Then make sure that the QDRO includes survivorship language for you in the event of your ex-husband's death. You should contact the plan administrator to ask it whether your share of the benefits is *protected* against your ex-husband's death either before or after his retirement. Get a copy of the QDRO approval letter from the plan, and keep it.

2. Your Ex-Husband Died before the QDRO Was Done: What Do You Do Now?

Let's assume that the worst does happen. You find out that your ex-husband has died and that no QDRO was ever prepared in your case. Unfortunately, with the current state of the law, there may be no quick fix in this situation. Plan administrators may be well within their rights to reject a QDRO submitted after the death of the participant. According to them, at the moment of your ex-husband's death, the plan's only obligation was to pay survivor benefits to an *eligible* surviving spouse. Alternatively, they would be obligated to pay a survivor annuity to a former spouse in accordance with the terms of a QDRO that was on file with the plan administrator at the time of the former spouse's death. If your ex-husband was single when he died and there was no QDRO on file granting survivor rights to any former spouse, the plan's obligation to pay a pension on behalf of the participant ceases immediately.

However, the following actions (with no guarantee) could help secure benefits for you if your ex-husband dies before a QDRO is drafted:

(a) Review the terms of your original judgment entry of divorce or your separation agreement to determine whether it could be construed as a QDRO in its own right. In other words, there is no legal requirement that a QDRO be a stand-alone document. If the written terms of your divorce decree were specific enough, the decree could be deemed to be a QDRO in the eyes of the plan administrator. There has been case law on this topic in the past, in which the parties' original divorce decree was approved by the plan administrator as a QDRO because it contained substantially all of the important information that must be in a QDRO.

(b) Determine whether any other people are entitled to survivor annuity benefits under the plan as a result of your ex-husband's death. In other words, if he had a new spouse who is eligible to receive a survivor benefit, it may not be too late to submit a QDRO that would award you a portion of that survivor annuity. But some plans do not permit this, and there is some case law that states that the survivor benefits can only vest in the new spouse to whom he was married on his retirement.

(c) Have your attorney attempt to draft a *nunc pro tunc* QDRO for you. The Latin term nunc pro tunc means *retroactive* or *now for then*. It refers to the court's inherent power to make the record speak the truth (to record what actually was done but was not recorded or was erroneously recorded). The court may decide that its intent on your divorce was to award you a portion of your ex-husband's pension benefits free and clear and not contingent on his continued survival. It intended to provide each party with a lifetime stream of income and to ensure that your ex-husband's death should not affect your continued rights to receive a portion of his pension benefits.

For this purpose, the plan administrator may accept a nunc pro tunc QDRO that is considered to be effective before your ex-husband's death. For example, if your ex-husband died on August 15, 2002, your attorney could prepare a nunc pro tunc QDRO backdated to August 1. If the judge signs this QDRO, the terms of the QDRO would be deemed effective on August 1, which is before your ex-husband died. Unfortunately, this is not a foolproof solution. Some judges may be reluctant to sign a nunc pro tunc QDRO, and some plan administrators may refuse to accept it. But there is case law in which this option has worked, and it's definitely worth a try.

Last, and probably least, is a malpractice suit against your divorce attorney for failing to draft a QDRO on a timely basis, especially if he or she agreed to prepare a QDRO for you when you divorced. In deference to the difficult task of divorce attorneys — an occupation that calls on them to be psychologist, family attorney, tax attorney, business attorney, trial litigator, and now pension attorney — I don't want to give the opinion that a malpractice suit should be your first recourse. It should only be your last. The standard of care for divorce attorneys in the arena of pensions and QDROs is not very high today. That is, a majority of divorce attorneys are still very intimidated and confused by QDROs. And if that's the norm rather than the exception, a favorable outcome for you in a malpractice suit is not automatic. In other words, the court may feel the attorney's pain. That is why your first line of defense is a good offense. If your ex-husband is still alive, get the QDRO done now to avoid this potential nightmare situation.

∘♀

CHAPTER 14

You Are Going Through a Divorce (What Should You Know about the QDRO Process?)

Don't let your attorney rely on the use of a company-provided model QDRO. Because so many attorneys are intimidated by the QDRO process, many are willing to take whatever the company gives them and simply fill in the blanks. I will say it again: Don't allow your attorney to do this. Your ex-husband's company does not give a damn about your rights to share in his pension benefits. And reading the company's model QDROs should help make this point obvious. If your attorney doesn't understand the intricacies of the QDRO process, make sure that he or she hires an expert who does.

1. Complete Discovery of All Plans of Coverage

Your attorney needs to make sure that he or she has discovered all of the plans in which your ex-husband participated during the marriage. This may not be as easy as you think. Most employees are not familiar with the defined benefit pension plan. And you may not realize that while your ex-husband participated in the company's 401(k) plan, he also participated in its employee stock ownership plan. Your attorney may either take a deposition from your ex-husband or send a subpoena to the plan administrator asking it to verify all plans of coverage.

2. The Separation Agreement: Making Sure Your Attorney Doesn't Shortchange Your QDRO Rights

Many attorneys properly draft QDROs that include such essential features as a coverture formula, preretirement and postretirement survivorship rights, cost of living adjustments (COLAs), early retirement subsidies, and other "value-added benefits" to protect the co-ownership interests of the nonparticipant spouse. Although this may be equitable from a marital property perspective, it could pose a large problem if the parties' separation agreement does not refer to these value-added benefits. The separation agreement is the document that sets forth which marital items will belong to your ex-husband and which items you get to keep. This is also the document in which your attorney should emphasize your rights to a portion of your ex-husband's pension benefits.

Many attorneys, having read thousands of separation agreements over the years, fall flat on their face when it comes to including proper language regarding the equitable division of the pension benefits. All too often, the parties' separation agreement contains only one sentence about the division of the retirement benefits, such as: "The wife shall receive one-half of the husband's pension; QDRO shall issue." This statement can be catastrophic. It's tantamount to stating elsewhere in the separation agreement: "The wife and husband have a joint checking account at XYZ Bank with a balance of $200,000. It is agreed that the wife shall get some of it." Or, "The wife and husband own two cars, a 1974 Chevy Vega and a 1998 BMW 740iL. It is agreed that the wife shall get one of them." As ridiculous as these examples sound, the single sentence regarding the division of pension benefits is just as vague and just as dangerous. The term "one-half of the husband's pension benefits" can be interpreted in many ways. Further, there is no mention of other pension benefit rights that should be afforded to the alternate payee under a QDRO, such as those mentioned in the preceding paragraph.

If your attorney does not draft the QDRO immediately while your divorce is pending, and your soon-to-be ex-husband is covered under an ERISA-governed defined benefit pension plan, your separation agreement should at the very least address the following specific QDRO issues.

2.1 Calculation of assigned benefit: Coverture recommended

The separation agreement should specify exactly how the alternate payee's share of the benefit is to be determined. To provide the alternate payee with inflationary protection, you should use the following coverture language:

> *The alternate payee (i.e., the Wife) is hereby granted the right to receive a portion of the participant's (i.e., the Husband's) pension benefits in an amount equal to the actuarial equivalent of **Fifty Percent (50%) of the Marital Portion of the participant's Accrued Benefit** under the Plan as of the participant's benefit commencement date, or the Alternate Payee's benefit commencement date, if earlier. The Marital Portion shall be determined by multiplying the participant's Accrued Benefit by a fraction (less than or equal to 1.0), the numerator of which is the number of months of the participant's participation in the Plan earned during the marriage (**from ____to____**), and the denominator of which is the total number of months of the participant's participation in the Plan as of the earlier of his date of cessation of benefit accruals or the date that alternate payee commences her benefits hereunder.*

In this way, the alternate payee's share of the benefit is not "frozen" as of the date of divorce, but the years of service used in the calculation of the participant's accrued benefit are still based solely on the amount of service accrued during the marriage. Remember, under a defined benefit pension plan, neither a participant nor an alternate payee is entitled to any interest or investment earnings under the plan. The only way to provide an alternate payee with some inflationary protection is to utilize the *marital portion* or *coverture* approach. Chapter 7 includes a detailed discussion of the coverture approach.

2.2 Survivorship protection

You should include language that will provide the alternate payee with Qualified Preretirement Survivor Annuity (QPSA) coverage if the participant dies before the alternate payee's benefit commencement date, but only with respect to survivor benefits attributable to the marital portion of the participant's accrued benefit. This is necessary to secure the alternate payee's rights to the assigned portion of the pension. Any remaining survivor annuity benefits could become payable to a subsequent spouse of the plan participant.

Again, there are two types of survivor annuity benefits under an ERISA-governed defined benefit pension plan. One is the QPSA discussed above. The second is called the Qualified Joint and Survivor Annuity (QJSA). This reduced, postretirement surviving spouse annuity becomes payable if the participant predeceases a spouse *after* retirement. Under federal law, this form of benefit is usually the automatic form of payment for married participants. Just as with the QPSA, this postretirement QJSA coverage can be provided to an alternate payee under a QDRO.

However, the postretirement QJSA survivorship protection may not be necessary (or equitable) if you use the separate interest approach for your QDRO, in which the alternate payee's benefits are actuarially adjusted to that person's life expectancy. Under the separate interest approach (discussed in Chapter 3), the death of the participant after the alternate payee's benefit commencement date will have no effect on the alternate payee's continued receipt of the benefits. Therefore, because the alternate payee is assured of a lifetime of benefits (once they commence), it is generally not necessary to include this postretirement QJSA protection in the QDRO.

2.3 Postretirement cost of living adjustments

You may also want to include language in the separation agreement that provides the alternate payee with a pro rata share of any postretirement cost of living increases attributable to the marital portion of the participant's benefits. If this is your intent for the QDRO, be sure to include this in your separation agreement.

2.4 Early retirement subsidy

Your separation agreement should also include language that provides you with a pro rata share of any employer-provided "early retirement subsidy" granted to the participant on the date of that person's retirement. (See Section 8 of Sample 8.) Not understanding the early retirement subsidy provisions of the plan can also be catastrophic for the alternate payee. It can mean the difference between receiving $300 per month for life or $1,500 per month for life. (See Chapter 8 for a complete description of the effects of the early retirement subsidy on QDROs.) Remember, under most defined benefit pension plans, employees are enticed into taking early retirement before their normal retirement age. These enticements come in the form of early retirement incentives known as the early retirement subsidy. In essence, the plan provides the participant with unreduced or slightly reduced pension benefits even though he is retiring before his normal retirement age of 65. These subsidies can be huge. Some plans will provide unreduced, or just slightly reduced pensions as early as age 50, even though the normal retirement age under the plan is 65. At the time of divorce, the participant may be just one or two years away from being eligible for the subsidy. Therefore, don't be fooled into accepting a QDRO without the early retirement subsidy language. As a co-owner of the pension, you should be entitled to a pro rata share of the early retirement subsidy.

Also remember that the early retirement subsidy only becomes payable when the participant retires early under the plan. It is not available to an alternate payee who decides to commence her share of the benefits before the participant actually retires. So, your QDRO should therefore include *recalculation* language in case your ex-husband subsequently retires early after you have already started receiving your share of the pension. This language is perfectly acceptable to the vast majority of the thousands of plan administrators I have dealt with. Many plan administrators have even built this recalculation language into their own model QDROs. Again, read Chapter 8 in its entirety to better understand how the subsidy works.

2.5 Anti-circumvention language

Never underestimate the savvy of a plan participant to circumvent the provisions of the divorce decree. It's true that your ex-husband once loved you, but my guess is, if he could figure out a way to keep you from getting your fair share of his pension benefits, he will do it. Therefore, it is always a good idea to include the following language to help protect against detrimental actions by the participant. I refer to this protective language as *anti-circumvention* language. It is meant to prevent your ex-husband from circumventing the provisions of your judgment entry. This language is also helpful in case of a plan termination or if the plan trustee mistakenly paid your assigned share of the benefits to your ex-husband:

Constructive Receipt: *In the event that the Plan Trustee inadvertently pays to the Participant any benefits that are assigned to the Alternate Payee pursuant to the terms of this Order, the Participant shall immediately reimburse the Alternate Payee to the extent that he has received such benefit payments, and shall forthwith pay such amounts so received directly to the Alternate Payee within ten (10) days of receipt.*

Continued Jurisdiction: *The Court shall retain jurisdiction with respect to this separation agreement and the QDRO to the extent required to maintain its qualified status and the original intent of the parties as stipulated herein. The Court shall also retain jurisdiction to enter such further orders as are necessary to enforce the assignment of benefits to Alternate Payee as set forth herein, including the recharacterization thereof as a division of benefits under another plan, as applicable, or to make an award of alimony or spousal support, if applicable, in the event that Participant fails to comply with the provisions contained above requiring said payments to Alternate Payee.*

Plan Termination: *In the event that the Plan is terminated, whether on a voluntary or involuntary basis, and the Participant's benefits become guaranteed by the Pension Benefit Guaranty Corporation (PBGC), the Alternate Payee's benefits, as stipulated herein, shall also be guaranteed to the same extent in accordance with the Plan's termination rules and in the same ratio as the Participant's benefits are guaranteed by the PBGC.*

Actions by Participant: *The Participant shall not take any actions, affirmative or otherwise, that can circumvent the terms and provisions of this Qualified Domestic Relations Order, or that could diminish or extinguish the rights and entitlements of the Alternate Payee as set forth herein. Should the Participant take any action or inaction to the detriment of the Alternate Payee, he shall be required to make sufficient payments **directly** to the Alternate Payee to the extent necessary to neutralize the effects of his actions or inactions and to the extent of the Alternate Payee's full entitlements as set forth hereunder.*

3. Incorporate the QDRO by Reference into Your Decree

Since QDROs have been in existence for more than 15 years now, there really is no excuse for not preparing the QDRO concurrently with the divorce proceeding. As the late coach Woody Hayes said about his Ohio State football team when defending his "three yards and a cloud of dust" mentality: "If you throw the football, three things can happen, and two of them are bad." Of course, he was referring to the possibility of an incompletion or interception. Unfortunately, the same logic applies to QDROs. If your attorney does not prepare the QDRO at the same time as the divorce or include comprehensive QDRO-type language in the separation agreement, 14 things can happen to you, and 13 of them are bad. For example, if a QDRO is not drafted and approved by the company at the time of or immediately after the divorce, you could face one or more of the following situations:

- Lose all of your pension if the participant dies
- Lose your rights to a preretirement survivor annuity
- Lose your rights to a postretirement survivor annuity
- Lose your rights to separate interest lifetime pension if participant retires
- Lose your rights to postretirement COLA enhancements
- Lose your rights to a coverture based pension
- Lose your rights to early retirement subsidy
- Miss months or years of pension payments if the participant retires without informing you
- Lose your investment gains on a 401(k) plan
- Lose your entire 401(k) assignment if the participant quits and takes distribution
- Lose your entire 401(k) assignment if the participant dies
- Lose your rights to name the beneficiary upon your own death
- Lose your rights to direct your own plan investments under a 401(k) plan

It should be obvious to all attorneys today what the adverse consequences can be if the QDRO is not prepared in a timely fashion. Ideally, your attorney should prepare the QDRO at the same time as the separation agreement and then *incorporate it by reference* directly into the agreement. If he or she does this, there will be no confusion down the road, nor will you have to deal with an irate attorney (for the participant) when you try to include this language in a QDRO-drafted later. If you do not incorporate the QDRO by reference, you must, at the very least, include comprehensive and definitive language in the separation agreement that clarifies the division of the participant's retirement benefits.

4. Don't Forget the Boilerplate

Very few, if any, model QDROs prepared by plan administrators contain adequate language to protect the alternate payee from detrimental actions of the participant or from a QDRO that does not really carry out the parties' intentions. Your QDRO should include anti-circumvention language for this purpose. See the beginning of this chapter for a discussion of the required language, such as reservation of jurisdiction, actions by the participant, and termination of the plan. Although your QDRO would certainly be approved without this language, it's certainly better to include it just in case of the unforeseen. It may be necessary to go back to court to straighten out your assignment of benefits in case the worst does happen. The Samples in Chapter 19 contain provisions that are recommended for helping to secure the alternate payee's share of the benefits.

5. Follow-Through with the Plan Administrator

Once your attorney drafts the QDRO for you, it is imperative that you follow through with the plan administrator to be sure that your QDRO is approved. Don't leave this up to your attorney. Once your case is over, he or she will not be inclined to do much more work for you. And it could take the plan administrator many months to review your QDRO. Also, once the plan administrator does approve your QDRO, you should read its interpretation/approval letter carefully. It is quite possible that the plan administrator's interpretation of the QDRO does not coincide with your intent. Also, if the plan administrator does not send you a detailed interpretation of the QDRO along with its approval letter, you may want to inquire about certain provisions of the QDRO to ensure that your rights are guaranteed, especially with respect to survivor rights. You must make sure that the premature death of your ex-husband will not extinguish your rights to a lifetime of pension income.

CHAPTER 15

Your Attorney Never Drafted a QDRO for You (Is This Considered Malpractice? What Are Your Options Now?)

Although pension benefits accrued by plan participants have been considered marital assets for several decades, they were extremely difficult to divide before 1984. If your divorce occurred before 1984, it is likely that your divorce decree did not award you a portion of your ex-husband's pension benefits. It's also highly unlikely that you can do anything about it today. But if your divorce occurred after 1984 (the year that QDROs were created), you should have been awarded a portion of your ex-husband's pension benefits. Obviously, there is a standard of care issue to consider here. Most attorneys are still not very familiar with the QDRO provisions of the law today, so you can imagine what their level of knowledge was in the middle to late 1980s — almost nonexistent. During the infancy period of QDROs, it is likely that the entire pension issue was overlooked when the attorneys were battling to divide the parties' marital assets. This situation is much different today; often the biggest issue during a divorce is not who gets the kids, but who gets the pension?

There should be no excuse for a divorce attorney in the 1990s or later forgetting about the pension benefits accrued by your ex-husband during the marriage. These benefits should have been considered a marital asset subject to equitable distribution on divorce. During your marriage, if your ex-husband worked for a company that maintained a pension or savings plan, you should have been awarded a portion of the plan(s) when you divorced. If not, this should be considered malpractice by your attorney, especially when the pension benefits might be the largest marital asset.

Unfortunately, it is difficult to reopen a divorce case to redistribute the property settlement. But before you consider a malpractice suit against your former divorce attorney, you may want to hire an attorney to try to reopen your case. If you can show that your ex-husband concealed the existence of his pension plan, the court may reconsider the property settlement. In some jurisdictions, it may be relatively easy to reopen a case. Some courts believe that a property settlement is not final until the pension issue is presented and equitably divided.

If you find out that it's too late to reopen your case, a malpractice suit may be your only option. You, of course, have to weigh the burden of the costs and aggravation of such a lawsuit against the benefits of winning. Your attorney may have to hire an expert at evaluating pension plans to place a present value on the portion of the pension benefits that should have been awarded to you at divorce. If you were only married to your ex-husband for a relatively short time, the costs of a malpractice lawsuit will probably outweigh the value of the pension benefits that you would have realized with a properly drafted settlement agreement.

1. Failure to Draft a QDRO

If your divorce occurred in the middle to late 1980s, check to see if you were awarded a portion of your ex-husband's pension benefits. If your separation agreement did award you a portion of the pension benefits, you should determine whether a QDRO was prepared and submitted to the plan administrator. And then you must determine whether it was "approved" by the plan administrator. You can find this out by contacting the plan administrator (the company's personnel or benefits department) and asking it if it ever approved a QDRO in your case. If the answer is no, now is the time to get it done. Contact an attorney and ask him or her to draft and finalize the QDRO process for you. Since it's likely that the attorney you contact will not be an expert with QDROs, you may want to use an appropriate sample QDRO contained in this book. You and your attorney may want to review the various sample QDROs together. This could help reduce your legal expenses and assure you of a lifetime of pension income.

Remember, it's generally not too late to draft a QDRO if your ex-husband is still working. You can draft a separate interest QDRO and secure for yourself a lifetime of pension income. But if your ex-husband either retired or died, it may be too late to draft a QDRO providing you with a lifetime stream of income. This is where the QDRO issue gets difficult. If your ex-husband has already retired, you can still draft a QDRO to receive a portion of each monthly pension check. But remember, a company will generally only accept a shared payment QDRO once the participant has retired. This means that you can receive your share of the monthly payments for only as long as your ex-husband is alive and receiving a pension. Difficult as it may be, you must hope that your ex-husband lives a long and healthy life. Alternatively, you could consider a malpractice suit against your divorce attorney for not drafting the QDRO on a timely basis. If you are considering a malpractice suit, do not wait for your ex-husband to die. A lawsuit today could potentially buy you a term life insurance policy to protect your assigned share of the pension benefits against your ex-husband's premature death.

2. Be Proactive

If you find out that a QDRO was never drafted for you, the time to do it is now. There are no special time limits for preparing a QDRO (other than your ex-husband still being alive and still having rights to receive benefits in the plan). Don't rely on anyone else. Contact a divorce attorney immediately or use one of the sample QDROs in this book. I recommend that you do both: hire an attorney and use, with his or her assistance, one of the appropriate sample QDROs in this book. I cannot guarantee that the sample QDROs in Chapter 19 will be accepted by every plan administrator in the country on the first go-around, but these QDROs should provide a good basis for securing a lifetime interest in your ex-husband's pension or savings plan benefits.

3. Consider a Malpractice Suit a Last Resort

Consider a malpractice suit against your original divorce attorney only as a last resort. Your first order of business should be to draft the QDRO now and get it through the plan administrator. If your ex-husband has not yet retired, it's not too late for you to receive your full share of the pension benefits via a properly drafted QDRO. I know of many cases in which the former spouse's first instinct was to initiate a lawsuit against her attorney, only to find out later that she could have spent just a few hundred dollars to draft a QDRO and secure her pension rights.

This book is not intended to be a guide to malpractice suits against divorce attorneys. Its single goal is to educate the public regarding the importance of QDROs. A properly drafted QDRO is the only way to secure for the nonparticipant spouse a very significant property right — *the pension*. But if your attorney dropped the ball and never drafted a QDRO for you, and you find out that it's now too late to draft one (because your ex-husband has retired, has died, or has already received a full pension distribution), then a malpractice suit against your attorney may be justified.

CHAPTER 16

What If Your Ex-Husband Is Covered under the Federal Civil Service Retirement System?

If your ex-husband is employed by the federal government, he is covered under one of two federally administered defined benefit pension plans. One is called the Civil Service Retirement System (CSRS). The other is the Federal Employees Retirement System (FERS). This chapter focuses on coverage under the CSRS, but the sample court order that appears at the end of this chapter (see Sample 3) also applies if your ex-husband was covered under the FERS. Just be sure to change the name of the plan accordingly if you use this model court order.

Unfortunately, the federal government's plans are exempt from the QDRO provisions of the law. Remember, QDROs apply only to an ERISA-governed pension plan (a pension plan sponsored by a private employer). The federal government is not considered a private employer. But there is good news: the Office of Personnel Management (OPM), which is located in Washington, DC, administers both the CSRS and the FERS. It will honor its own version of a QDRO, which is called a Court Order Acceptable for Processing (COAP).

A COAP functions just like a QDRO. It too is a court order that must be signed by a judge and submitted to the OPM for review and approval.

Three types of retirement benefits are payable by the OPM:

- An *employee annuity* (a monthly pension benefit payable to your ex-husband when he retires)

- A *refund of employee contributions* (payable if your ex-husband quits employment before his retirement)

- A *survivor annuity* (payable to a surviving spouse or a former spouse under a COAP, upon your ex-husband's death)

Since the OPM administers each type of retirement benefit independently, it is extremely important to address each one of these benefits separately under a COAP.

You should have been awarded a portion of your ex-husband's pension benefits in your divorce decree if he worked for the federal government at any time during your marriage. And your attorney should have prepared a COAP for you at the time of your divorce and submitted it to the OPM in Washington, DC, for review and approval. If these events did not occur, take care of this situation right away. Just as is the case with QDROs for private employer plans, you must be sure that a COAP is drafted and approved by the OPM. And also like QDROs, divorce attorneys throughout the country are typically unfamiliar with the proper drafting of COAPs. It is in your best interests to be proactive here so that you do not forfeit your rights to this very valuable marital asset. The following sections outline some critical issues to consider when drafting a court order to divide a federal civil service pension benefit.

1. Dividing the Employee Annuity

The following questions are important to consider when the employee annuity is to be divided.

1.1 What are the employee eligibility requirements?

For a former spouse to be entitled to a portion of the employee annuity, several requirements must first be met by the employee. The employee must —

- be separated from a position in federal service covered by the CSRS or the FERS,

- apply for the payment of the employee annuity, and

- be entitled to the immediate commencement of his or her employee annuity.

The employee annuity is the lifetime pension that your ex-husband will receive when he retires from either the CSRS or the FERS.

1.2 What are the maximum allowable payments to the former spouse?

Under a COAP, the payments to a former spouse may not exceed 100 percent of the employee's *net annuity*. The net annuity is the amount of monthly annuity payable to an employee after deducting from the gross annuity any of the following amounts owed —

- by the retiree to the United States,

- for health insurance premiums,

- for life insurance premiums,

- for Medicare premiums, or

- for federal or state income tax purposes.

1.3 Are there any application requirements for the former spouse?

There are application requirements for the former spouse. When a COAP is submitted to the OPM, the former spouse (or his or her legal representative) must also submit an application letter. No special form is required, but the application letter must be accompanied by the following documents and information:

- A certified copy of the COAP that is directed at the employee annuity

- A certification from the former spouse or the former spouse's representative that the COAP is currently in force and has not been amended, superseded, or set aside

- Information sufficient for the OPM to identify the employee or retiree, such as his or her full name, the CSRS or the FERS claim number, date of birth, and social security number

- The current mailing address of the former spouse

- If the employee has not retired under the CSRS or the FERS or has died, the mailing address of the employee

Also, if payments to the former spouse under a COAP are to be terminated if the former spouse remarries, no payment will be made to the former spouse until he or she submits to the OPM a statement certifying —

- that a remarriage has not occurred;
- that the former spouse will notify the OPM within 15 calendar days of the occurrence of any remarriage; and
- that the former spouse will be personally liable for any overpayment to him or her resulting from a remarriage.

1.4 When do payments to a former spouse terminate?

The employee annuity payments to a former spouse under a COAP will generally stop at your death or your ex-husband's death, which ever occurs first. However, your share of the payments could continue past your death if the COAP expressly provides that the former spouse's share of the employee annuity should continue to either the retiree's children or to your estate. Alternatively, the COAP could include language requiring your share of the benefits to revert to your ex-husband when you die.

2. The Refund of Employee Contributions

The following questions are important when considering refunds of employee contributions.

2.1 What amounts are subject to a court order acceptable for processing?

A former spouse of a separated employee who has separated from a covered position in the federal civil service, before being eligible to retire and begin receiving an employee annuity, may receive up to 100 percent of the refund of employee contributions. Your ex-husband must be entitled to an immediate refund of his contributions and must apply for the payment of this refund.

2.2 Will the payment of a refund of employee contributions terminate any future rights to a portion of the employee annuity or a survivor annuity?

If a separated employee and/or a former spouse applies for and receives a refund of employee contributions, all future rights that either party may have for an employee annuity or a survivor annuity will be terminated. This is true even if the employee receives all of the refund. Therefore, if there is a COAP in place that provides you with a portion of the employee annuity, your rights to a portion of this employee annuity will be forever lost if your ex-husband receives a refund of employee contributions.

2.3 Can a COAP prevent a separated employee from receiving a refund of employee contributions, in order to secure a former spouse's future right to a portion of an employee annuity or a former spouse survivor annuity?

It is possible to bar the payment of a refund of employee contributions to a separated employee. Two conditions must be met, though. First, the COAP must expressly direct the OPM not to pay a refund of employee contributions; second, this court order, or a prior COAP, must award the former spouse a portion of the employee annuity or a former spouse survivor annuity.

3. Former Spouse Survivor Annuities

The Office of Personnel Management must comply with COAPs that award *former spouse survivor annuities* as a result of divorce, an annulment of marriage, or a legal separation of employees covered under the CSRS or the FERS.

3.1 What are the maximum survivor benefits payable under the Civil Service Retirement System?

Under the CSRS, the maximum possible former spouse survivor annuity payable to a former spouse is 55 percent of the employee annuity, unless the surviving spouse or former spouse was married to the retiree at retirement and agreed to a lesser amount at that time.

3.2 Are there eligibility requirements for the former spouse?

For a former spouse to be eligible for a former spouse survivor annuity, he or she must have been married for at least nine months to an employee or retiree who performed at least 18 months of civilian service covered by the CSRS and whose marriage to the employee or retiree ended before the death of the employee or retiree. Also, the former spouse must apply to receive these benefits.

Remarriage before age 55: It is important to remember that a former spouse survivor annuity or the right to a future former spouse survivor annuity based on a COAP will terminate in accordance with the terms of the COAP, but in no event later than the last day of the month before the former spouse remarries before age 55 or dies. In other words, if your COAP provides you with a former spouse survivor annuity, you will not see any of it upon your ex-husband's death if you remarry before your 55th birthday.

3.3 Do you have a future right to a former spouse survivor annuity?

There are special timing requirements for court orders that provide a former spouse with survivorship protection. A court order awarding a former spouse survivor annuity will not become a COAP if it is issued after the date of retirement or death of the employee and modifies or replaces the first order dividing the marital property of the employee or retiree and the former spouse. Therefore, your attorney should include the appropriate survivor language in your COAP to avoid any adverse circumstances, such as your ex-husband's retirement before the COAP is drafted.

3.4 How does the employee or former spouse pay for the cost of providing a former spouse survivor annuity under a COAP?

The only acceptable way to pay for the costs associated with providing a former spouse with a former spouse survivor annuity under a COAP is by *annuity reduction*. That is, the employee annuity will be reduced by the appropriate amount required to provide a former spouse survivor annuity. Alternatively, the COAP may provide that the cost of providing the survivor annuity will be deducted solely from the former spouse's share of the employee annuity.

3.5 Once a court order acceptable for processing has been prepared, where should it be sent?

If the court order is delivered by the United States Postal Service, it should be sent to the following address:

> Office of Personnel Management
> Retirement and Insurance Group
> P.O. Box 17
> Washington, DC 20044-0017

If the court order is delivered by process servers, express carriers, or other forms of hand-carried delivery, it should be sent to the following address:

> Court-ordered Benefits Section
> Allotments Branch
> Retirement and Insurance Group
> Office of Personnel Management
> 1900 E Street, NW
> Washington, DC

3.6 Can court orders bar the payment of employee annuities?

State courts cannot prevent the OPM from paying employee annuities to those entitled under the Civil Service Retirement System. Further, the OPM will not honor a COAP that purports to delay or otherwise prevent the payment of employee annuities at the time or in the amount required by statute.

The OPM will, however, honor a COAP that directs the OPM to pay all or a portion of the employee annuity to the court, an officer of the court acting as a fiduciary, or a state or local government agency during a divorce or legal separation proceeding.

3.7 What kind of formulas can be used in a COAP to identify the former spouse's share of the employee annuity?

To be acceptable to the OPM, the COAP may only use language that provides sufficient instructions and information that, from the face of the COAP, enable the OPM to compute the amount of the former spouse's benefits. The following alternatives are acceptable:

- A fixed-dollar amount

- A percentage or a fraction of the employee annuity

- A pro rata share (All things being equal, this is the recommended approach for dividing the pension benefits. It is the same as the coverture approach for QDROs. The term *pro rata share* means 50 percent of the fraction whose numerator is the number of months of federal civilian and military service that the employee performed during the marriage and whose denominator is the total number of months of federal civilian and military service performed by the employee. This marital fraction approach is a simple and convenient way to structure a COAP when referring to the former spouse's entitlement. When using this approach, the COAP must include the employee's date of marriage to the former spouse.)

- A formula that does not contain any variables whose values are not determinable from the face of the order or from the OPM files (Normal OPM files include information such as the dates of employment for all periods of creditable civilian and military service and the rate of basic pay for all periods of service.)

Sample 3 is a model COAP for use by you or your attorney, if your ex-husband participated under the Civil Service Retirement System. The pro rata approach is used in this model COAP. This approach is the equivalent of the coverture approach for QDROs discussed in Chapter 7. The COAP also provides you with a pro rata share of any survivor annuity benefits that may become payable in the event of your ex-husband's death. You or your attorney may find it necessary to modify this model language so that it conforms to the intent of the parties and your negotiated settlement agreement.

SAMPLE 3
MODEL COURT ORDER ACCEPTABLE FOR PROCESSING (COAP) UNDER THE CIVIL SERVICE RETIREMENT SYSTEM

IT IS HEREBY ORDERED, ADJUDGED, AND DECREED AS FOLLOWS:

1. Effect of this Order as a Court Order Acceptable for Processing: This Order creates and recognizes the existence of a Former Spouse's right to receive a portion of the Employee's benefits payable under the Civil Service Retirement System ("CSRS"). Such benefits may represent a portion of the Employee Annuity or a Refund of Employee Contributions or may award a Former Spouse Survivor Annuity to the Former Spouse. It is intended to constitute a Court Order Acceptable for Processing under final regulations issued by the Office of Personnel Management ("OPM"). The provisions of this court order are drafted in accordance with the terminology used in Part 838 of Title 5, Code of Federal Regulations.

2. Employee Information: The name, last known address, social security number, and date of birth of the Employee are:

Name: _____("Employee")

Address: _____

Social Security Number: _____

Date of Birth:_____

3. Former Spouse Information: The name, last known address, social security number, and date of birth of the Former Spouse are:

Name: _____("Former Spouse")

Address: _____

Social Security Number: _____

Date of Birth:_____

The Former Spouse shall have the duty to notify the OPM in writing of any changes in his or her mailing address subsequent to the entry of this Order.

4. Identification of Retirement System: The Employee will be eligible for retirement benefits under the Civil Service Retirement System based on employment with the United States Government.

5. For Provision of Marital Property Rights: This Order relates to the provision of marital property rights and/or spousal support to the Former Spouse as a result of the [Order of Divorce] [Annulment of Marriage] between the Employee and the Former Spouse issued on_____.

6. Providing for Payments to Former Spouse: The Former Spouse is entitled to a portion of the Employee's Gross Monthly Annuity under the Civil Service Retirement System as set forth below. The United States Office of Personnel Management is hereby directed to pay the Former Spouse's share directly to the Former Spouse.

SAMPLE 3 — Continued

7. Amount of Former Spouse's Benefit: This Order assigns to the Former Spouse an amount equal to Fifty Percent (50%) of the Marital Portion of the Employee's Gross Monthly Annuity (including any military benefits paid by the OPM) determined as of the Employee's date of retirement. For the purposes of calculating the Former Spouse's share of the Employee's benefit, the Marital Portion shall be determined by multiplying the Employee's Gross Monthly Annuity by a fraction (less than or equal to 1.0), the numerator of which is the total number of months of Creditable Service earned under the CSRS during the marriage (from_____ to), and the denominator of which is the total number of months of the Employee's Creditable Service accrued under the Civil Service Retirement System (including military service credited to the CSRS, should the Employee opt out of receiving his military retired pay). The marriage began on _____.

In addition to the above, when COLAs are applied to the Employee's retirement benefits, the same COLA shall apply to the Former Spouse's share. Further, any salary adjustments that occur after the date of the divorce decree and before the Employee's date of retirement shall be incorporated into the calculation of the Former Spouse's share of the Employee Annuity.

With respect to the Former Spouse's share of the Employee's Gross Monthly Annuity, such portion shall be calculated without regard to any amounts that are withheld from the Employee's annuity for any reason (other than amounts withheld for the purpose of providing a Former Spouse Survivor Annuity).

8. Benefit Commencement Date: The Former Spouse shall commence her or his benefits as soon as administratively feasible following the date this Order is approved as a Court Order Acceptable for Processing, or on the date the Employee commences his or her benefits, if later. Payments shall continue to the Former Spouse for the remainder of the Employee's lifetime. However, in the event that the Former Spouse dies before the Employee, the United States Office of Personnel Management is directed to pay the Former Spouse's share of the Employee's civil service retirement benefits to her or his "estate." The Employee agrees to arrange or to execute all forms necessary for the OPM to commence payments to the Former Spouse in accordance with the terms of this Order.

9. Refund of Employee Contributions: If the Employee leaves the federal service before retirement and applies for a refund of employee contributions under the CSRS, the Former Spouse shall be entitled to a pro rata share of the refund of such employee contributions.

10. Former Spouse Survivor Annuity: Pursuant to Section 8341(h)(1) of Title 5, United States Code, the Former Spouse shall be awarded a Former Spouse Survivor Annuity under the Civil Service Retirement System equal to a "pro rata share." Further, the costs associated with providing this Former Spouse Survivor Annuity coverage shall be divided equally between the Former Spouse and the Employee.

The Employee agrees to take all necessary steps to elect the Former Spouse as the designated beneficiary for purposes of establishing and sustaining such surviving spouse coverage for the Former Spouse.

11. Transfer to the FERS: In the event that the Employee makes a one-time irrevocable election to transfer into the Federal Employees Retirement System ("FERS") before his retirement, then the

Former Spouse shall be entitled to a portion of the Employee's Basic Annuity and/or a Refund of Employee Contributions under the FERS calculated in a manner similar to that enumerated in Sections 7 and 9 above for the CSRS annuity and refund, respectively, and payable directly from the FERS. Additionally, the Former Spouse shall be entitled to a Former Spouse Survivor Annuity payable under the FERS and determined in a manner similar to the survivor benefits set forth under Section 10 above. Further, such Former Spouse Survivor Annuity shall be payable directly from the FERS. **(Note: You may delete this section entirely, if your ex-husband is covered under the FERS at the time you draft this order.)**

12. Savings Clause: This Order is not intended to, and shall not be construed in such a manner as to, require the OPM:

(a) to pay a Former Spouse a portion of an Employee Annuity before the employee annuity begins to accrue;

(b) to pay a Former Spouse any amounts that are in excess of an Employee's net annuity; or

(c) to pay a Former Spouse Survivor Annuity in excess of the maximum permitted amounts under the CSRS and the FERS.

13. Constructive Receipt: In the event that the CSRS inadvertently pays to the Employee any benefits that are assigned to the Former Spouse pursuant to the terms of this Order, the Employee shall immediately reimburse the Former Spouse to the extent that he or she has received such benefit payments, and shall forthwith pay such amounts so received directly to the Former Spouse within ten (10) days of receipt.

14. Continued Jurisdiction: The Court shall retain jurisdiction with respect to this Order to the extent required to maintain its status as a Court Order Acceptable for Processing and the original intent of the parties as stipulated herein. Further, the Court shall retain jurisdiction to enter such further orders as are necessary to enforce the award to Former Spouse of the benefits awarded herein, including the recharacterization thereof as a division of benefits earned under another retirement system in lieu of the retirement benefits under CSRS or other benefits received in lieu of CSRS retirement benefits, or to make an award of alimony in the event that the Employee fails to comply with the provisions contained above requiring said payments to Former Spouse by any means.

15. Actions by Employee: If the Employee takes any action that prevents, decreases, or limits the collection by the Former Spouse of the sums to be paid hereunder, he or she shall make payments to the Former Spouse directly in an amount sufficient to neutralize, as to the Former Spouse, the effects of the actions taken by the Employee.

16. Notice of Pending Retirement: The Employee shall be required to notify the Former Spouse, in writing, within thirty (30) days prior to his or her actual date of retirement. Such notice shall indicate his or her intentions to retire and his or her elected benefit commencement date. The notice shall be sent via regular, first class mail. For this purpose, the Former Spouse shall notify the Employee of any changes in the Alternate Payee's mailing address.

CHAPTER 17

What If Your Ex-Husband Is Covered under a Military Retirement Plan?

The Uniformed Services Former Spouse's Protection Act (Public Law 97-252) became effective on February 1, 1983. Former spouses of military members were now permitted to receive a portion of the military retired pay in accordance with the terms of the divorce decree. The act recognizes the right of state divorce courts to require the appropriate administrative agency of the military to make direct payments to a former spouse of up to 50 percent of the member's disposable retired pay. Dividing military retired pay may be more complex than drafting QDROs for ERISA-governed plans. There are some limitations and timing requirements of which you and your attorney must be aware. This chapter briefly outlines some of the important issues to consider when drafting a court order to divide military retired pay. If your ex-husband was covered by a military pension plan at any time during your marriage, your divorce decree should have awarded you a share of his military retired pay. The plan administrator for the military pension plan, the Defense Finance and Accounting Service (DFAS), located in Cleveland, Ohio, administers court orders to divide retired pay.

1. The 10/10 Rule for Property Divisions

It is critical for you and your attorney to understand the 10/10 Rule before drafting an order to divide a member's retired pay. If the 10/10 Rule is not satisfied, the military may not be required to honor a court order to divide the member's retired pay. It is defined as follows:

> *If the spouse or former spouse to whom payments are to be made under this section was not married to the member for a period of 10 years or more during which the member performed at least 10 years of service creditable in determining the member's eligibility for retired pay, payments may not be made under this section to the extent that they include an amount resulting from the treatment by the court under subsection (c) of disposable retired pay of the member as property of the member or **property** of the member and his spouse. [emphasis added]*

What this simply means is that if your marriage lasted for less than ten years, forget about drafting an order that directs the military to provide you with any direct payments of your ex-husband's retired pay. DFAS will not honor the court order. Further, if you were married for more than ten years but the member did not earn at least ten years of creditable service during the marriage, DFAS will also not honor your court order to divide the retired pay.

Note that the 10/10 Rule only applies to a property division. *It is not applicable to a division of retired pay for alimony (spousal support) or child support purposes.* You may still submit a court order to DFAS for the purposes of child support or alimony even if the 10/10 Rule was not satisfied. DFAS will honor the court order to provide direct payments of alimony or child support.

2. Maximum Payments to a Former Spouse

Unlike a QDRO, which can provide an alternate payee with up to 100 percent of the participant's accrued pension benefits, under the military's pension plan there are limits on providing former spouse's with a portion of the member's disposable retired pay. The total amount of the disposable retired pay of a member payable under all court orders *may not exceed 50 percent* of the member's disposable retired pay.

However, in cases where there is both a division of disposable retired pay and a *garnishment* to enforce the collection of child support and/or alimony, the total amount payable cannot exceed 65 percent of such retired pay.

When the court order is completed and certified by the court, it should be sent to DFAS for its review at the following address:

DFAS, Cleveland Center (Code LF)
(For Former Spouse Annuity Purposes)
P.O. Box 998002
Cleveland, Ohio 44199-8002

A government form known as DFAS FORM 2293 should be completed by you and submitted along with a certified copy of the court order. DFAS will accept copies; an original form is not required. Simply fill out the form as requested and return it with the court order. You can obtain a copy of the form by contacting DFAS in Cleveland, Ohio.

3. The Military Uses Only the Shared Payment Approach

Another limitation on dividing military retired pay is the fact that the military will not actuarially adjust your share of the benefits to your own life expectancy. It will not accept a separate interest type of order, which is a common QDRO approach under ERISA-governed defined benefit pension plans. Therefore, you begin to receive your share of the disposable retired pay only when your ex-husband retires and his benefits start. Further, you can only continue to receive your assigned share of the benefits until either your death or the member's death, whichever occurs first, unless the order includes Survivor Benefit Plan (SBP) protection for you. (See section **5.** later in this chapter.)

Although it is not expressly stated in the statute, the military has also been accepting coverture-style language to define the former spouse's share of the retired pay. However, DFAS will not calculate the actual numerator of the coverture fraction. Your order must include the actual number of years and months of the member's creditable service earned during the marriage. If you simply include the duration of the marriage and ask DFAS to calculate the numerator, it will reject your court order. DFAS will, however, calculate the denominator of the coverture fraction, which represents the member's total creditable service at retirement. You may use the following language, as applicable, if your intent is to utilize the coverture approach.

> *This Order assigns to Former Spouse an amount equal to* **Fifty Percent (50%) of the Marital Portion of the Participant's disposable retired pay** *under the Plan as of his benefit commencement date. The Marital Portion shall be determined by multiplying the Member's disposable retired pay by a fraction, the numerator of which is the number of months of the Member's creditable service in the Plan earned during the marriage* **(which shall be defined as [_____] months)**, *and the denominator of which is the total number of months of the Member's creditable service in the Plan as of his date of retirement.*

Likewise, if you use the coverture approach for a member of the *reserves*, the numerator of the coverture fraction should equal the "points" accumulated by the member during the marriage. A reservist's retired pay is not based on years of accumulated service, but is rather based on a point system. This is necessary due to the part-time nature of a reservist's career. DFAS will calculate the denominator of the coverture fraction which, of course, represents the member's total points accumulated at retirement. You or your attorney will have to request the number of points accumulated by your ex-husband during the marriage in order for you to complete the numerator of the coverture fraction.

4. The Soldiers' and Sailors' Civil Relief Act of 1940

If you are preparing a court order to divide military retired pay and the member is not yet retired and in pay status, your order must include express language certifying that the member's rights under the Soldiers' and Sailors' Civil Relief Act of 1940 (50 U.S.C. App. Section 501 et seq.) were observed. Essentially, this shows that the member was actually "in town" and aware of the division of retired pay and was represented by counsel or consented to the division of benefits during the divorce proceeding. The following language in the decree should suffice for this purpose:

Observance of Member's Rights Under the Soldiers' and Sailors' Civil Relief Act of 1940: The Member's rights under the Soldiers' and Sailors' Civil Relief Act of 1940 (50 U.S.C. App. Section 521) were observed by the Court as evidenced by [his presence at the proceedings], [the presence of his legal counsel at the proceedings], or [his affirmative signature on the divorce decree and/or separation agreement]. (Use one or more.)

5. Survivor Benefit Plan (SBP) Coverage for a Former Spouse

The only way to provide a former spouse with continued benefit payments after the death of the member is through the Survivor Benefit Plan (SBP). If your order does not include SBP protection, your share of the benefits will cease at the member's death. There are several restrictions on the SBP plan, so you and your attorney must pay special attention to this portion of the plan when preparing a court order to divide military retired pay.

The court order may require a member to elect (or enter into an agreement to elect) SBP coverage for the former spouse. That is, a member may elect to provide an SBP survivor annuity to a former spouse. Any such election to provide a former spouse with SBP coverage would prevent any payments of the survivor annuity to a current spouse or child. There is a time limit on the election of former spouse SBP coverage by the member. Any such election must be written, signed by the member, and received by the secretary (DFAS) within one year after the date of the decree of divorce, dissolution, or annulment.

When making the election for former spouse SBP coverage, the member must disclose whether this election of the former spouse coverage was required. The disclosure statement must be in writing and signed by the member and it must set forth:

(a) whether the election is being made pursuant to the requirements of a court order; or

(b) whether the election is being made pursuant to a written agreement previously entered into voluntarily by such person as a part of, or incident to, a proceeding of divorce, dissolution, or annulment and (if so) whether such voluntary written agreement has been incorporated in, or ratified or approved by, a court order.

6. Deemed Election of Former Spouse Coverage

Even if the member is required to elect SBP coverage for the former spouse pursuant to the terms of a divorce decree, this coverage may be lost for the former spouse if the member fails to make the election on a timely basis. In order to help secure your rights to SBP coverage, you may bring about a *deemed election* for this coverage in case your ex-husband fails or refuses to make such an election.

There is a separate time limit for the former spouse to make a deemed election on behalf of the member. Any deemed election may be honored only if DFAS receives it within *one year* of the date of the court order or filing involved.

You and your attorney should never assume that your ex-husband will make the required SBP election in a timely manner. To best secure your rights to a potential survivor annuity in the event of your ex-husband's death, you should sign off on the following deemed election language, or similar language, and submit it to DFAS concurrently with the submission of the court order to divide the military retired pay:

Deemed SBP Election Notice

I request that the United States Defense Finance and Accounting Service ("DFAS") "deem" an election by [name of member], [Social Security Number of member], that I, [name of former spouse], [Social Security Number of former spouse] be the beneficiary of [name of member's] survivor annuity under the Survivor Benefit Plan ("SBP") as set forth under the court order dated _____. By order of the Court of Common Pleas, Division of Domestic Relations, _____ County, _____, dated _____, a court of competent jurisdiction, the agreement of [name of member] and [name of former spouse] was approved. In accordance with 10 U.S.C. Section 1450(f), I request that DFAS name me as the beneficiary of [name of member's] survivor benefit annuity.

It is also important for you and your attorney to understand that DFAS has a separate department that handles the SBP survivorship benefits. Therefore, if your court order includes SBP coverage, I suggest that you send a *second copy* of the court order and the "Deemed SPB Election Notice" to the following address:

DFAS, Cleveland Center
(For SBP Survivor Annuity Purposes)
P.O. Box 99191
Cleveland, Ohio 44199-8002

7. Termination of SBP Surviving Spouse Coverage on the Remarriage of a Former Spouse before Age 55

It is important to understand that you will lose your rights to a survivor annuity under the SBP portion of the plan if you are remarried to any individual before you reach the age of 55. However, if you remarry before reaching age 55 and that marriage is ended by death, annulment, or divorce, the payment of the SBP survivor annuity will resume on the first day of the month in which the marriage ends. But to carry this one step further, if you are also entitled to an annuity under the SBP as a result of the subsequent marriage to another military member, you may not receive both annuities; you must choose which one to receive.

8. Anti-Circumvention Language

Because of the possibility that a former spouse may lose rights to a portion of the member's retired pay for reasons beyond the former spouse's control, such as the member opting for disability pay in lieu of retired pay, your court order should include the following *anti-circumvention* language to help secure your share of the benefits against detrimental actions by your ex-husband. Please add to or delete from the following sections. Also, please understand that the following language is not intended for administration by DFAS. They will ignore the following language. Its only intent is to require the participant or the court, whichever is applicable, to help carry out the intent of the parties.

> ***Merger of Benefits and Indemnification:*** *The Member agrees not to merge the Member's disposable military retired pay with any other pension and not to pursue any*

course of action that would defeat the Former Spouse's right to receive a portion of the disposable military retired pay of the Member. The Member agrees not to take any action by merger of the military retirement pension so as to cause a limitation in the amount of the total retired pay in which the Member has a vested interest and, therefore, the Member will not cause a limitation of the Former Spouse's monthly payments as set forth above. The Member agrees to indemnify Former Spouse for any breach of this paragraph as follows: If the Member becomes employed or otherwise has his military pension merged, which employment or other condition causes a merger of the Member's disposable military retired pay, the Member will pay to the Former Spouse directly the monthly amount provided to Former Spouse above, under the same terms and conditions as if those payments were made pursuant to the terms of this order.

Direct Payment by Member: *If in any month, direct payment is not made to Former Spouse by DFAS (or the appropriate military pay center) pursuant to the terms of this Order, Member shall pay the amounts called-for above directly to Former Spouse by the fifth day of each month in which the military pay center fails to do so, beginning on the date that Former Spouse would have otherwise been entitled to commence her payments. This includes any amounts received by the Member in lieu of disposable retired pay, including but not limited to, any amounts waived by Member in order to receive Veterans Administration (ie: disability) benefits or any amounts received by Member as a result of an early-out provision, such as VSI or SSB benefits.*

Actions by Member: *If the Member takes any action that prevents, decreases, or limits the collection by the Former Spouse of the sums to be paid hereunder, he shall make payments to the Former Spouse directly in an amount sufficient to neutralize, as to the Former Spouse, the effects of the actions taken by the Member.*

Continued Jurisdiction: *The Court shall retain jurisdiction to enter such further orders as are necessary to enforce the award to spouse of the military retirement benefits awarded herein, including the recharacterization thereof* *as a division of Civil Service or other retirement benefits, or to make an award of alimony (in the sum of benefits payable plus future cost of living adjustments) in the event that the Member fails to comply with the provisions contained above requiring said payments to the Former Spouse by any means, including the application for a disability award or filing of bankruptcy, or if military or government regulations or other restrictions interfere with payments to the Former Spouse as set forth herein, or if the Member fails to comply with the provisions contained above requiring said payments to the Former Spouse.*

Although the above language is complex, it is critical to you securing your share of the retired pay. *Hire an attorney to help you with the appropriate court order to divide your ex-husband's military retired pay.* You may also need assistance in completing the necessary Form 2293 and the "Deemed Election" notice to secure your rights to a survivor annuity. I can't emphasize enough how difficult it is to secure your rights to your ex-husband's military retired pay. Do hire an attorney for this purpose. It is also likely that your divorce attorney will have to hire his or her own expert to help with this process because of the complexities associated with dividing military pension benefits.

9. Model Military Court Orders to Divide Retired Pay

The following samples contain model court orders that you or your attorney may use to divide your ex-husband's military pension benefits. If he was an active member of the military, use Sample 4. If he was a member of the reserves, use Sample 5, and if he is already retired and receiving his pension benefits, use Sample 6.

These orders may be more difficult to understand than a traditional QDRO for a regular employer-sponsored pension plan. The standard boilerplate protective language included in the models is necessary to secure your share of the benefits and is rather complex. It may be in your best interests to hire an attorney if your ex-husband was covered by a military pension at any time during your marriage. Although your attorney will probably not be very familiar with the procedures for securing your share of the military pension, he or she can certainly help you understand some of the issues covered in this chapter and in the model court orders included on the following samples.

SAMPLE 4
MILITARY QUALIFYING COURT ORDER
(For active members)

IT IS HEREBY ORDERED AS FOLLOWS:

I. SUBSTANTIVE PROVISIONS

1. Acknowledgment: The parties acknowledge that [*Member's Name*] is currently accruing a military retirement benefit based on his or her service in the [*Branch of Military*]. The parties further agree that his or her former spouse, [*Former Spouse's Name*], has an interest in such military retirement benefits, and shall receive from [*Member's*] disposable military retired pay an amount as set forth below. Further, [*Member*] shall assist [*Former Spouse*] in submitting any application(s) necessary to secure her or his share of his or her disposable military retired pay as awarded herein.

2. Member Information:

The "Member" as referred to herein is _____

Address: _____

Social Security Number: _____

3. Former Spouse Information:

The "Former Spouse" is referred to herein is _____

Address: _____

Social Security Number: _____

The Former Spouse and Member were married on: _____

4. Assignment of Benefits: The Member assigns to the Former Spouse an interest in the Member's disposable military retired pay. The Former Spouse is entitled to a direct payment in the amount specified below and shall receive payments at the same times as the Member.

5. Observance of Member's Rights Under the Soldier's and Sailor's Civil Relief Act of 1940: The Member's rights under the Soldier's and Sailor's Civil Relief Act of 1940 (50 App U.S.C. Section 521) were observed by the Court as evidenced by [CHOOSE ONE OR MORE OF THE FOLLOWING] [*his or her presence at the proceedings*], [*the presence of his or her legal counsel at the proceedings*], or [*his or her affirmative signature on the divorce decree and/or separation agreement*].

6. Amount of Payments:

[Alternative 1: Coverture Approach] This Order assigns to the Former Spouse an amount equal to **Fifty Percent (50%) of the Marital Portion of the Member's disposable military retired pay** under the Plan as of his or her benefit commencement date. The Marital Portion shall be determined by multiplying the Member's disposable military retired pay by a fraction (less than or equal to 1.0), the numerator of which is the number of months of the Member's creditable military service in the Plan earned during the marriage **(which shall be defined as _____months)**, and the denominator of which is the total number of months of the Member's creditable military service in the Plan as of his or her date of retirement.

[Alternative 2: Fixed-Dollar Approach] This Order assigns to the Former Spouse a portion of the Member's disposable military retired pay in the amount of **$ _____per month**.

[Alternative 3: Percentage of Final Pension] This Order assigns to the Former Spouse an amount equal to ____ % of the Member's disposable military retired pay.

[Alternative 4: Frozen Percentage] The Former Spouse shall receive _____% of the disposable military retired pay the Member would have received had the Member retired at the rank of _____ with _____years of creditable service.

[Optional Cost of Living Adjustment Language When Using Percentage Only]

In addition to the above, the Former Spouse (*CHOOSE ONE*) [*shall/shall not*] receive a proportionate share of any postretirement **cost of living adjustments ("COLA")** made to the Member's benefits on or after the date of his or her retirement.

7. SURVIVOR BENEFIT PLAN ("SBP") PROTECTION FOR FORMER SPOUSE:

The Court hereby orders that the Former Spouse shall be treated as the Member's irrevocable beneficiary under the Survivor Benefit Plan ("SBP"). The Member shall be required to make the necessary election in a timely manner to effectuate the SBP coverage for the Former Spouse and shall execute such paperwork as is required. The level of SBP coverage required for the Former Spouse shall be that which will provide her or him with the same benefit payments after the Member's death that she or he was eligible to receive or receiving before his or her death.

8. Duration of Payments: The monthly payments set forth under Paragraph 6 shall commence to the Former Spouse as soon as administratively feasible following the commencement of Member's disposable retired pay and shall continue during the joint lives of the parties, and, to the extent permitted under law, irrespective of the future marital status of either of them; they shall terminate only upon the death of either the Member or the Former Spouse.

9. Jurisdiction: The jurisdictional requirements of 10 U.S.C. Section 1408 have been complied with, and this order has not been amended, superseded, or set aside by any subsequent order.

10. Duration of Marriage Acknowledgment (Compliance with 10/10 Rule): The Member and the Former Spouse acknowledge that they have been married for a period of more than ten years, during which time the Member performed more than ten years of creditable military service. The parties were married from _____ **to** _____ .

II. MISCELLANEOUS PROVISIONS

11. Overpayments: The Former Spouse agrees that any future overpayments to her or him are recoverable and subject to involuntary collection from her or his estate.

12. Notification: The Former Spouse agrees to notify DFAS about any changes in this Qualifying Court Order or the order affecting these provisions of it, or in the eligibility of any recipient receiving benefits pursuant to it.

13. Qualification: The Member and the Former Spouse intend that this order qualify under the Uniformed Services Former Spouses' Protection Act, 10 U.S.C. Section 1408 and following. All provisions shall be construed and modified to the extent necessary in order to qualify as a Qualifying Court Order.

14. Continued Cooperation of Member: The Member agrees to cooperate with the Former Spouse to prepare an application for direct payment to the Former Spouse from the Member's retired or retainer pay pursuant to 10 U.S.C. Section 1408. The Member agrees to execute all documents that the **[branch of military]** may require to certify that the disposable military retired pay can be provided to the Former Spouse.

15. Merger of Benefits and Indemnification: The Member agrees not to merge the Member's disposable military retired pay with any other pension and not to pursue any course of action that would defeat the Former Spouse's right to receive a portion of the disposable military retired pay of the Member. The Member agrees not to take any action by merger of the military retirement pension so as to cause a limitation in the amount of the total retired pay in which the Member has a vested interest and, therefore, the Member will not cause a limitation of the Former Spouse's monthly payments as set forth above. If the Member becomes employed or otherwise has his or her military pension merged, which employment or other condition causes a merger of the Member's disposable military retired pay, the Member will pay to the Former Spouse directly the monthly amount provided in Paragraph 6, under the same terms and conditions as if those payments were made pursuant to the terms of this order.

16. Direct Payment by Member: If in any month, direct payment is not made to the Former Spouse by DFAS (or the appropriate military pay center) pursuant to the terms of this Order, the Member shall pay the amounts called for above directly to the Former Spouse by the fifth day of each month in which the military pay center fails to do so, beginning on the date that the Former Spouse would have otherwise been entitled to commence her or his payments. This includes any amounts received by the Member in lieu of disposable retired pay, including but not limited to, any amounts waived by Member in order to receive Veterans Administration (disability) benefits or any amounts received by the Member as a result of an early-out provision, such as VSI or SSB benefits.

17. Actions by Member: If the Member takes any action that prevents, decreases, or limits the collection by the Former Spouse of the sums to be paid hereunder, he or she shall make payments to Former Spouse directly in an amount sufficient to neutralize, as to the Former Spouse, the effects of the actions taken by the Member.

SAMPLE 4 — Continued

18. Submission of Information: The parties acknowledge that the following items must be sent by the Former Spouse to DFAS (Cleveland Center), located at P.O. Box 998002, Cleveland, Ohio 44199-8002. The Member agrees to provide any of this information to the Former Spouse at the Former Spouse's request and to make all necessary efforts to obtain any of this information that the Former Spouse is unable to obtain.

(a) A copy of this Qualifying Court Order that divides retired pay and any decree that approves this order certified within ninety (90) days immediately preceding its service on the applicable military pay center for the [*Branch of Military*].

(b) A statement by the Former Spouse verifying that the divorce decree has not been modified, superseded, or set aside.

(c) The parties' marriage certificate.

(d) The Member's name, social security number, date of birth, and the name of the military service.

(e) The Former Spouse's name, address, and social security number.

19. Continued Jurisdiction: The Court shall retain jurisdiction to enter such further orders as are necessary to enforce the award to spouse of the military retirement benefits awarded herein, including the recharacterization thereof as a division of Civil Service or other retirement benefits, or to make an award of alimony in the event that the Member or DFAS fails to comply with the provisions contained above requiring said payments to the Former Spouse by any means, including the application for a disability award or filing of bankruptcy, or if military or government regulations or other restrictions interfere with payments to the Former Spouse as set forth herein.

20. Taxes: The Former Spouse shall be liable for any federal, state, or local income taxes associated with her or his assigned share of the disposable military retired pay.

21. Discovery: The Member hereby waives any privacy or other rights as may be required for the Former Spouse to obtain information relating to the Member's date and time of retirement, last unit assignment, final rank, grade and pay, present or past retired pay, or other such information as may be required to enforce the award made herein, or required to revise this order so as to make it enforceable.

22. Notice of Pending Retirement: The Member shall be required to notify the Former Spouse, in writing, within thirty (30) days prior to his or her actual date of retirement. Such notice shall indicate his or her intentions to retire and his or her elected benefit commencement date. The notice shall be sent via regular, first class mail. For this purpose, the Former Spouse shall notify the Member of any changes in her or his mailing address.

23. Definition of military retirement: For the purposes of interpreting this Court's intention in making the division set out in this Order and for the purpose of calculating the amount due the former spouse, "military retirement" includes retired pay paid or to which the Member would be entitled for

SAMPLE 4 — Continued

longevity of active duty and/or reserve component military service and all payments paid or payable under the provisions of Chapter 38 or Chapter 61 of Title 10 of the United States Code, before any statutory, regulatory, or elective deductions are applied. For purposes of calculating the Former Spouse's share of the benefits awarded to her or him by the Court, the marital property interests of the Former Spouse shall also include a pro rata share of all amounts the Member actually or constructively waives or forfeits in any manner and for any reason or purpose, including, but not limited to, any waiver made in order to qualify for Veterans Administration or disability benefits. It also includes a pro rata share of any sum taken by the Member in lieu of or in addition to his or her disposable retired pay, including, but not limited to, exit bonuses, voluntary separation incentive pay (VSI), special separation benefit (SSB), or any other form of retirement benefits attributable to separation from military service. Such pro rata share shall be based on the same formula, percentage, or amounts specified in Section 6 above, as applicable. In the event that the DFAS will not pay the Former Spouse directly all or a portion of the benefits awarded to her or him herein, then the Member shall be required to pay her or him directly in accordance with the terms and provisions set forth in Section 16 above.

IT IS SO ORDERED.

_____

JUDGE (*Enter Judge*)

SAMPLE 5
MILITARY QUALIFYING COURT ORDER
(For reservists)

IT IS HEREBY ORDERED AS FOLLOWS:

I. SUBSTANTIVE PROVISIONS

1. Acknowledgment: The parties acknowledge that [*Member's Name*] is currently accruing a military retirement benefit based on his or her service in the [*Branch of Military*]. The parties further agree that his or her former spouse, [*Former Spouse's Name*], has an interest in such military retirement benefits, and shall receive from [*Member's*] disposable military retired pay an amount as set forth below. Further, [*Member*] shall assist [*Former Spouse*] in submitting any application(s) necessary to secure her or his share of his or her disposable military retired pay as awarded herein.

2. Member Information:

The "Member" as referred to herein is _____

Address: _____

Social Security Number: _____

3. Former Spouse Information:

The "Former Spouse" is referred to herein is _____

Address: _____

Social Security Number: _____

The Former Spouse and Member were married on: _____

4. Assignment of Benefits: The Member assigns to the Former Spouse an interest in the Member's disposable military retired pay. The Former Spouse is entitled to a direct payment in the amount specified below and shall receive payments at the same times as the Member.

5. Observance of Member's Rights Under the Soldier's and Sailor's Civil Relief Act of 1940: The Member's rights under the Soldier's and Sailor's Civil Relief Act of 1940 (50 U.S.C. App. Section 521) were observed by the Court as evidenced by [*CHOOSE ONE OR MORE OF THE FOLLOWING*] [*his or her presence at the proceedings*], [*the presence of his or her legal counsel at the proceedings*], or [*his or her affirmative signature on the divorce decree and/or separation agreement*].

6. Amount of Payments:

[**Alternative 1: Coverture Approach**] This Order assigns to the Former Spouse an amount equal to **Fifty Percent (50%) of the Marital Portion of the Member's disposable military retired pay** under the Plan as of his or her benefit commencement date. The Marital Portion shall be determined by multiplying the Member's disposable military retired pay by a fraction (less than or equal to 1.0), the numerator of which is the number of points accumulated by the Member during the marriage (**which shall be defined as _____ points**), and the denominator of which is the total number of points accumulated by the Member as of his or her date of retirement.

[Alternative 2: Fixed-Dollar Approach] This Order assigns to the Former Spouse a portion of the Member's disposable military retired pay in the amount of **$_____ per month**.

[Alternative 3: Percentage of Final Pension] This Order assigns to the Former Spouse an amount equal to ___ % of the Member's disposable military retired pay.

[Alternative 4: Frozen Percentage Approach] The Former Spouse shall receive _____% of the disposable military retired pay the Member would have received had the Member become eligible to receive military retired pay on _____ **(USE MEMBER'S AGE 60 DATE)** at the rank of _____ with _____ reserve retirement points and_____ years of service for basic pay purposes.

[Optional Cost of Living Adjustment Language When Using Percentage Only]

In addition to the above, the Former Spouse (*CHOOSE ONE*) [*shall/shall not*] receive a proportionate share of any post-retirement **cost of living adjustments ("COLA")** made to the Member's benefits on or after the date of his or her retirement.

7. SURVIVOR BENEFIT PLAN ("SBP") PROTECTION FOR FORMER SPOUSE:

The Court hereby orders that the Former Spouse shall be treated as the Member's irrevocable beneficiary under the Survivor Benefit Plan ("SBP"). The Member shall be required to make the necessary election in a timely manner to effectuate the SBP coverage for the Former Spouse and shall execute such paperwork as is required. The level of SBP coverage required for the Former Spouse shall be that which will provide her or him with the same benefit payments after the Member's death that she or he was eligible to receive or receiving before his or her death.

8. Duration of Payments: The monthly payments set forth under Paragraph 6 shall commence to the Former Spouse as soon as administratively feasible following the commencement of Member's disposable retired pay and shall continue during the joint lives of the parties, and, to the extent permitted under law, irrespective of the future marital status of either of them; they shall terminate only upon the death of either the Member or the Former Spouse.

9. Jurisdiction: The jurisdictional requirements of 10 U.S.C. Section 1408 have been complied with, and this order has not been amended, superseded, or set aside by any subsequent order.

10. Duration of Marriage Acknowledgment (Compliance with 10/10 Rule): The Member and the Former Spouse acknowledge that they have been married for a period of more than ten years during which time the Member performed more than ten years of creditable military service. The parties were married from _____ **to** _____ .

SAMPLE 5 — Continued

II. MISCELLANEOUS PROVISIONS

11. Overpayments: The Former Spouse agrees that any future overpayments to her or him are recoverable and subject to involuntary collection from her or his estate.

12. Notification: The Former Spouse agrees to notify DFAS about any changes in this Qualifying Court Order or the order affecting these provisions of it, or in the eligibility of any recipient receiving benefits pursuant to it.

13. Qualification: The Member and the Former Spouse intend that this order qualify under the Uniformed Services Former Spouses' Protection Act, 10 U.S.C. Section 1408 and following. All provisions shall be construed and modified to the extent necessary in order to qualify as a Qualifying Court Order.

14. Continued Cooperation of Member: The Member agrees to cooperate with the Former Spouse to prepare an application for direct payment to the Former Spouse from the Member's retired or retainer pay pursuant to 10 U.S.C. Section 1408. The Member agrees to execute all documents that the **[branch of military]** may require to certify that the disposable military retired pay can be provided to the Former Spouse.

15. Merger of Benefits and Indemnification: The Member agrees not to merge the Member's disposable military retired pay with any other pension and not to pursue any course of action that would defeat the Former Spouse's right to receive a portion of the disposable military retired pay of the Member. The Member agrees not to take any action by merger of the military retirement pension so as to cause a limitation in the amount of the total retired pay in which the Member has a vested interest and, therefore, the Member will not cause a limitation of the Former Spouse's monthly payments as set forth above. If the Member becomes employed or otherwise has his or her military pension merged, which employment or other condition causes a merger of the Member's disposable military retired pay, the Member will pay to the Former Spouse directly the monthly amount provided in Paragraph 6, under the same terms and conditions as if those payments were made pursuant to the terms of this order.

16. Direct Payment by Member: If in any month, direct payment is not made to the Spouse by DFAS (or the appropriate military pay center) pursuant to the terms of this Order, the Member shall pay the amounts called for above directly to the Former Spouse by the fifth day of each month in which the military pay center fails to do so, beginning on the date that the Former Spouse would have otherwise been entitled to commence her or his payments. This includes any amounts received by the Member in lieu of disposable retired pay, including but not limited to, any amounts waived by the Member in order to receive Veterans Administration (disability) benefits or any amounts received by Member as a result of an early-out provision, such as VSI or SSB benefits.

17. Actions by Member: If the Member takes any action that prevents, decreases, or limits the collection by the Former Spouse of the sums to be paid hereunder, he or she shall make payments to the Former Spouse directly in an amount sufficient to neutralize, as to the Former Spouse, the effects of the actions taken by the Member.

18. Submission of Information: The parties acknowledge that the following items must be sent by the Former Spouse to DFAS (Cleveland Center), located at P.O. Box 998002, Cleveland, Ohio 44199-8002. The Member agrees to provide any of this information to the Former Spouse at the Former Spouse's request and to make all necessary efforts to obtain any of this information that the Former Spouse is unable to obtain.

(a) A copy of this Qualifying Court Order that divides retired pay and any decree that approves this order certified within ninety (90) days immediately preceding its service on the applicable military pay center for the **United States Army Reserves**.

(b) A statement by the Former Spouse verifying that the divorce decree has not been modified, superseded, or set aside.

(c) The parties' marriage certificate.

(d) The Member's name, social security number, date of birth, and the name of the military service.

(e) The Former Spouse's name, address, and social security number.

19. Continued Jurisdiction: The Court shall retain jurisdiction to enter such further orders as are necessary to enforce the award to spouse of the military retirement benefits awarded herein, including the recharacterization thereof as a division of Civil Service or other retirement benefits, or to make an award of alimony in the event that the Member or DFAS fails to comply with the provisions contained above requiring said payments to the Former Spouse by any means, including the application for a disability award or filing of bankruptcy, or if military or government regulations or other restrictions interfere with payments to the Former Spouse as set forth herein.

20. Taxes: The Former Spouse shall be liable for any federal, state, or local income taxes associated with her or his assigned share of the disposable military retired pay.

21. Discovery: The Member hereby waives any privacy or other rights as may be required for the Former Spouse to obtain information relating to the Member's date and time of retirement, last unit assignment, final rank, grade and pay, present or past retired pay, or other such information as may be required to enforce the award made herein, or required to revise this order so as to make it enforceable.

22. Notice of Pending Retirement: The Member shall be required to notify the Former Spouse, in writing, within thirty (30) days prior to his or her actual date of retirement. Such notice shall indicate his or her intentions to retire and his or her elected benefit commencement date. The notice shall be sent via regular, first class mail. For this purpose, the Former Spouse shall notify the Member of any changes in her or his mailing address.

23. Definition of military retirement: For the purposes of interpreting this Court's intention in making the division set out in this Order and for the purpose of calculating the amount due the former spouse, "military retirement" includes retired pay paid or to which the Member would be entitled for longevity of active duty and/or reserve component military service and all payments paid or payable under the provisions of Chapter 38 or Chapter 61 of Title 10 of the United States Code, before any statutory, regulatory, or elective deductions are applied. For purposes of calculating the Former Spouse's share of the benefits awarded to her or him by the Court, the marital property interests of the Former Spouse shall also include a pro rata share of all amounts the Member actually or constructively waives or forfeits in any manner and for any reason or purpose, including, but not limited to, any waiver made in order to qualify for Veterans Administration or disability benefits. It also includes a pro rata share of any sum taken by the Member in lieu of or in addition to his or her disposable retired pay, including, but not limited to, exit bonuses, voluntary separation incentive pay (VSI), special separation benefit (SSB), or any other form of retirement benefits attributable to separation from military service. Such pro rata share shall be based on the same formula, percentage, or amounts specified in Section 6 above, as applicable. In the event that the DFAS will not pay the Former Spouse directly all or a portion of the benefits awarded to her or him herein, then the Member shall be required to pay her or him directly in accordance with the terms and provisions set forth in Section 16 above.

IT IS SO ORDERED.

_____

JUDGE (*Enter Judge*)

SAMPLE 6
MILITARY QUALIFYING COURT ORDER
(If currently retired)

IT IS HEREBY ORDERED AS FOLLOWS:

I. SUBSTANTIVE PROVISIONS

1. Acknowledgment: The parties acknowledge that [*Member's Name*] is currently receiving a military retirement benefit based on his or her service in the [*Branch of Military*]. The parties further agree that his or her former spouse, [*Former Spouse's Name*], has an interest in such military retirement benefits, and shall receive from [*Member's*] disposable military retired pay an amount as set forth below. Further, [*Member*] shall assist [*Former Spouse*] in submitting any application(s) necessary to secure her or his share of his or her disposable military retired pay as awarded herein.

2. Member Information:

The "Member" as referred to herein is _____

Address: _____

Social Security Number: _____

3. Former Spouse Information:

The "Former Spouse" is referred to herein is _____

Address: _____

Social Security Number: _____

The Former Spouse and Member were married on: _____

4. Assignment of Benefits: The Member assigns to the Former Spouse an interest in the Member's disposable military retired pay. The Former Spouse is entitled to a direct payment in the amount specified below and shall receive payments at the same times as the Member.

5. Amount of Payments:

[Alternative 1: Fixed-Dollar Approach] This Order assigns to the Former Spouse a portion of the Member's final disposable retired pay in the amount of **$ _____ per month**.

[Alternative 2: Percentage Approach] This Order assigns to the Former Spouse an amount equal to _____ **percent** of the Member's final disposable retired pay.

[Optional Cost of Living Adjustment Language When Using Percentage Only]

In addition to the above, the Former Spouse (*CHOOSE ONE*) (*shall/shall not*) receive a proportionate share of any post-retirement **cost of living adjustments ("COLA")** made to the Member's benefits on or after the date of this Order.

6. Duration of Payments: The Former Spouse shall begin to receive her or his share of the benefits as soon as administratively feasible following the date that this Order is approved by DFAS or the appropriate Military Pay Center. The Former Spouse shall continue to receive such benefits during the joint lives of the parties, and, to the extent permitted under law, irrespective of the future marital status of either of them; they shall terminate only upon the death of either the Member or the Former Spouse.

7. SURVIVOR BENEFIT PLAN ("SBP") PROTECTION FOR FORMER SPOUSE:

The Court hereby orders that the Former Spouse shall be treated as the Member's irrevocable beneficiary under the Survivor Benefit Plan ("SBP"). The Member shall be required to make the necessary election in a timely manner to effectuate the SBP coverage for the Former Spouse and shall execute such paperwork as is required. The level of SBP coverage required for the Former Spouse shall be that which will provide her or him with the same benefit payments after the Member's death that she or he was eligible to receive or receiving before his or her death.

8. Jurisdiction: The jurisdictional requirements of 10 U.S.C. Section 1408 have been complied with, and this order has not been amended, superseded, or set aside by any subsequent order.

9. Duration of Marriage Acknowledgment (Compliance with 10/10 Rule): The Member and the Former Spouse acknowledge that they have been married for a period of more than ten years, during which time the Member performed more than ten years of creditable military service. The parties were married from _____ **to** _____ .

II. MISCELLANEOUS PROVISIONS

10. Overpayments: The Former Spouse agrees that any future overpayments to her or him are recoverable and subject to involuntary collection from her or his estate.

11. Notification: The Former Spouse agrees to notify DFAS about any changes in this Qualifying Court Order or the order affecting these provisions of it, or in the eligibility of any recipient receiving benefits pursuant to it.

12. Qualification: The Member and the Former Spouse intend that this order qualify under the Uniformed Services Former Spouses' Protection Act, 10 U.S.C. Section 1408 and following. All provisions shall be construed and modified to the extent necessary in order to qualify as a Qualifying Court Order.

13. Continued Cooperation of Member: The Member agrees to cooperate with the Former Spouse to prepare an application for direct payment to the Former Spouse from the Member's retired or retainer pay pursuant to 10 U.S.C. Section 1408. The Member agrees to execute all documents that the **[branch of military]** may require to certify that the disposable military retired pay can be provided to the Former Spouse.

14. Merger of Benefits and Indemnification: The Member agrees not to merge the Member's disposable military retired pay with any other pension and not to pursue any course of action that would defeat the Former Spouse's right to receive a portion of the disposable military retired pay of the Member. The Member agrees not to take any action by merger of the military retirement pension so as to cause a limitation in the amount of the total retired pay in which the Member has a vested interest and, therefore, the Member will not cause a limitation of the Former Spouse's monthly payments as set forth above. If the Member becomes employed or otherwise has his or her military pension merged, which employment or other condition causes a merger of the Member's disposable military retired pay, the Member will pay to the Former Spouse directly the monthly amount provided in Paragraph 6, under the same terms and conditions as if those payments were made pursuant to the terms of this Order.

15. Direct Payment by Member: If in any month, direct payment is not made to spouse by DFAS (or the appropriate military pay center) pursuant to the terms of this Order, the Member shall pay the amounts called for above directly to the Former Spouse by the fifth day of each month in which the military pay center fails to do so, beginning on the date that the Former Spouse would have otherwise been entitled to commence her or his payments. This includes any amounts received by the Member in lieu of disposable retired pay, including but not limited to, any amounts waived by the Member in order to receive Veterans Administration (disability) benefits or any amounts received by Member as a result of an early-out provision, such as VSI or SSB benefits.

16. Actions by Member: If the Member takes any action that prevents, decreases, or limits the collection by the Former Spouse of the sums to be paid hereunder, he or she shall make payments to the Former Spouse directly in an amount sufficient to neutralize, as to the Former Spouse, the effects of the actions taken by the Member.

17. Submission of Information: The parties acknowledge that the following items must be sent by the Former Spouse to DFAS (Cleveland Center), located at P.O. Box 998002, Cleveland, Ohio 44199-8002. The Member agrees to provide any of this information to the Former Spouse at the Former Spouse's request and to make all necessary efforts to obtain any of this information that the Former Spouse is unable to obtain.

    (a)   A copy of this Qualifying Court Order that divides retired pay and any decree that approves this order certified within ninety (90) days immediately preceding its service on the applicable military pay center for the **[branch of military]**.

    (b)   A statement by the Former Spouse verifying that the divorce decree has not been modified, superseded, or set aside.

    (c)   The parties' marriage certificate.

    (d)   The Member's name, social security number, date of birth, and the name of the military service.

    (e)   The Former Spouse's name, address, and social security number.

18. Continued Jurisdiction: The Court shall retain jurisdiction to enter such further orders as are necessary to enforce the award to spouse of the military retirement benefits awarded herein, including the recharacterization thereof as a division of Civil Service or other retirement benefits, or to make an award of alimony in the event that the Member or DFAS fails to comply with the provisions contained above requiring said payments to the Former Spouse by any means, including the application for a disability award or filing of bankruptcy, or if military or government regulations or other restrictions interfere with payments to the Former Spouse as set forth herein.

19. Taxes: The Former Spouse shall be liable for any federal, state, or local income taxes associated with her or his assigned share of the disposable military retired pay.

20. Discovery: The Member hereby waives any privacy or other rights as may be required for the Former Spouse to obtain information relating to the Member's date and time of retirement, last unit assignment, final rank, grade and pay, present or past retired pay, or other such information as may be required to enforce the award made herein, or required to revise this order so as to make it enforceable.

21. Definition of Military Retirement: For the purposes of interpreting this Court's intention in making the division set out in this Order and for the purpose of calculating the amount due the former spouse, "military retirement" includes retired pay paid or to which the Member would be entitled for longevity of active duty and/or reserve component military service and all payments paid or payable under the provisions of Chapter 38 or Chapter 61 of Title 10 of the United States Code, before any statutory, regulatory, or elective deductions are applied. For purposes of calculating the Former Spouse's share of the benefits awarded to her or him by the Court, the marital property interests of the Former Spouse shall also include a pro rata share of all amounts the Member actually or constructively waives or forfeits in any manner and for any reason or purpose, including, but not limited to, any waiver made in order to qualify for Veterans Administration or disability benefits. It also includes a pro rata share of any sum taken by the Member in lieu of or in addition to his or her disposable retired pay, including, but not limited to, exit bonuses, voluntary separation incentive pay (VSI), special separation benefit (SSB), or any other form of retirement benefits attributable to separation from military service. Such pro rata share shall be based on the same formula, percentage, or amounts specified in Section 5 above, as applicable. In the event that DFAS will not pay the Former Spouse directly all or a portion of the benefits awarded to her or him herein, then the Member shall be required to pay her or him directly in accordance with the terms and provisions set forth in Section 15 above.

IT IS SO ORDERED.

_____

JUDGE (*Enter Judge*)

CHAPTER 18

What If Your Ex-Husband Is Covered under the Railroad Retirement Board Pension Plan?

If your ex-husband was a railroad employee, he is, in all likelihood, accruing a pension benefit under a federal pension plan known as the Railroad Retirement Board Pension Plan.

The Railroad Retirement Act is a federal law that provides retirement and disability annuities for qualified railroad employees, spouse annuities for their wives or husbands, and survivor benefits for the families of deceased employees. Regular railroad retirement annuities are calculated under a two-tiered formula consisting of two independent annuity segments: Tier I annuities and Tier II annuities.

1. A Tier I Annuity Is Not Divisible by a Court Order

The Tier I annuity is calculated in basically the same way as a Social Security benefit. It's based on railroad retirement credits and any non-railroad Social Security credits an employee has acquired. Although it is calculated using social Security formulas, it has railroad retirement age and service requirements. In other words, the Tier I component approximates what Social Security would pay if railroad work were covered under that system. As a result, to prevent the duplication of benefits, the Tier I annuity is reduced by the amount of any actual Social Security benefit paid on the basis of the participant's nonrailroad employment.

The Tier I annuity is not divisible by court order upon divorce. Therefore, you cannot receive any portion of your ex-husband's Tier I annuity.

2. A Tier II Annuity Is Divisible by a Court Order

The Tier II annuity is based on railroad retirement credits only and may be compared to the retirement benefits earned by workers in the private sector. Tier II represents the "pension" component of the annuity, similar to pension benefits earned by participants covered under ERISA-governed pension plans. The Railroad Retirement Board will honor a court order to divide the Tier II portion of your ex-husband's pension benefits under the Railroad Retirement Board Pension Plan. However, the following requirements must be met:

- The divorce decree must be final, and it must be issued in accordance with the laws of the jurisdiction of the court.

- The decree must provide for the division of the employee's benefits under the Railroad Retirement Act, as distinguished from payments under any private pension.

- The decree must provide for the division of the employee's benefits as part of a final disposition of property between the parties, rather than as an award of spousal support.

- The decree must obligate the Railroad Retirement Board rather than the employee to make direct payments to the former spouse.

- The decree may not divide the Tier I amount. The board applies a property award only to the employee's non-Tier I benefits without regard to the wording of the decree.

- The board's Bureau of Law in Chicago must receive a properly worded decree.

When dividing the Tier II annuity, you may use a fixed-dollar amount or a percentage. The Board will also accept the traditional *coverture* approach based on the ratio of the participant's service earned during the marriage divided by his total service at retirement. Also, unlike the situation under a QDRO, the nonparticipant spouse is not permitted to commence her share of the benefits until the participant actually retires and commences his benefits.

When the order is completed, you should send it via certified or registered mail, return receipt requested, or by personal service, to the following address:

Railroad Retirement Board
Bureau of Law
844 Rush Street
Chicago, Illinois 60611
Attn: Deputy General Counsel

Never refer to the word QDRO anywhere in the order. It may be rejected if you do. Call it something else, such as a Qualifying Court Order to Divide Railroad Retirement Benefits.

3. Vested Dual Benefit Payments and Supplemental Annuities

If an employee had qualified for dual benefits under both the railroad retirement system and Social Security before 1975 and meets certain vesting requirements, he or she can receive an additional annuity amount, which offsets, in part, the dual benefit reduction. This additional amount, which reflects the dual benefits payable before 1975, is called the *vested dual benefit payment*. This vested dual benefit payment may be considered for property division purposes in the same manner as the Tier II annuity.

Participants may also be eligible for a supplemental annuity in addition to their Tier II annuity and Vested Dual Benefit Payments. The supplemental annuity is relatively small, ranging from $25 to $43 per month, depending on years of service. Like the Tier II annuity and the vested dual benefit payment, the supplemental annuity may also be considered for property division purposes.

Therefore, when preparing a court order to divide the Tier II annuity, you should also include language that divides the vested dual benefit payments and the supplemental annuity, if any. Rather than specifying the Tier II component only, refer to the "total divisible portion" of the participant's benefits under the Railroad Retirement Board Pension Plan.

4. Survivor Rights to Tier II Annuities

Unlike the situation under a QDRO, you cannot receive any survivorship rights when dividing the Tier II annuity. This means that your share of the benefits will automatically cease when your ex-husband dies. However, you may be entitled to a survivor annuity from the Tier I portion of the participant's benefits in your own right, but only if you satisfy some stringent eligibility criteria (eight in all). This automatic annuity for eligible surviving former spouses is called the *divorced spouse annuity*. The list of requirements you must satisfy to receive this automatic survivor annuity are the following:

- The railroad employee is at least age 62 and is currently receiving a Railroad Retirement employee annuity.

- You are at least age 62 for a full month if applying for a reduced annuity, or at least age 65 if applying for an unreduced annuity.

- The marriage to the employee ended in a final decree of divorce.

- You were married to the employee for at least ten years immediately before the date the divorce became final.

- You are not currently married.

- You are not entitled to a Social Security benefit based on your own earnings, the amount of which before any reductions is greater than the maximum amount to which you would be entitled as a divorced spouse annuitant.

- You are not entitled to a spouse annuity, remarried widow(er)'s annuity, or surviving divorced spouse annuity on a different Railroad Retirement Board claim number, the net monthly rate of which is greater than the amount to which you would be entitled as a divorced spouse annuitant.

- You have stopped all work for pay for an employer covered by the Railroad Retirement Act, if any, and given up all rights to return to such service.

If you believe you have satisfied the above criteria, you should contact the Railroad Retirement Board to inquire about your divorced spouse annuity. You do not need to hire an attorney or prepare any special court order for this purpose.

5. Other Railroad Retirement Board Pension Plan Coverage

Many railroad employees who are entitled to receive retirement benefits from the Railroad Retirement Board may also be eligible for separate pension benefits from their employer. Many railroad companies offer supplemental pension plans for their employees. These are often defined benefit pension plans and are governed by ERISA, just as any other privately sponsored pension plan. Since these plans are subject to the QDRO provisions of the law, don't forget about your ex-husband's other potential plans of coverage. You or your attorney should send a discovery request to his employer asking whether he is covered under any retirement programs (defined benefit or defined contribution programs) in addition to his regular retirement benefits under the Railroad Retirement Board Pension Plan.

Sometimes these private employer plans are integrated with the railroad pension. In other words, any benefits accrued by the participant under the Railroad Retirement Board Pension Plan will be subtracted from the pension earned under the private employer's plan.

6. Model Court-Ordered Language to Divide the "Divisible Portion" of Railroad Retirement Benefits

Sample 7 may be used to divide the *divisible portion* of a railroad employee's retirement benefits. The divisible portion includes the Tier II annuity as well as any vested dual benefit payment or supplemental annuity payable to the participant. To the extent necessary, feel free to modify the following language to conform to the intent of your divorce decree. Also, note that the word QDRO does not appear anywhere in the order because it does not deal with an ERISA-governed plan here. Simply refer to the order as a Qualifying Court Order to Divide Railroad Retirement Benefits. If you call the order a QDRO, the Railroad Retirement Board may reject your order.

SAMPLE 7
MODEL QUALIFYING COURT ORDER TO DIVIDE RAILROAD RETIREMENT BENEFITS

IT IS HEREBY ORDERED AS FOLLOWS:

1. Acknowledgment: The parties acknowledge that [*name of employee*] currently has a vested interest in Railroad Retirement System benefits in accordance with the Railroad Retirement Act, based on his or her service with a Railroad Employer. The parties further agree that his or her former spouse, [*name of former spouse*], shall receive from [*name of employee's*] Railroad Retirement benefits an amount as set forth below. Further, [*name of employee*] shall assist [*name of former spouse*] in submitting any application(s) necessary to secure her or his share of the "divisible portion" of the Railroad Retirement benefits as awarded herein.

2. Employee Information:

The "Employee" as referred to herein is _____

Last known address: _____

Social Security Number: _____

3. Former Spouse Information:

The "Former Spouse" is referred to herein is _____

Last known address: _____

Social Security Number: _____

The Former Spouse and Employee were married on: _____

4. Assignment of Benefits: The Employee assigns to the Former Spouse an interest in his or her Railroad Retirement Benefits payable under the Railroad Retirement Act. The Former Spouse is entitled to "direct payments" of the amount that is specified in Section 5 below from the Railroad Retirement Board and that will be payable from the "divisible portion" of the Employee's Tier II Railroad Retirement Benefits (including any Vested Dual Benefit Payments or Supplemental Annuity).

The Former Spouse shall receive payments at the same times as the Employee.

5. Amount of Payments: The Former Spouse shall receive the following amount from each monthly payment of the Employee's "divisible portion" of his or her retirement benefits (the non-Tier I benefits):

The Former Spouse shall receive **Fifty Percent (50%)** of the Marital Portion of the Employee's Non-Tier I Railroad Retirement Benefits determined as of his or her date of retirement. (For this purpose, the Non-Tier I benefits shall include the Tier II Annuity, Vested Dual Benefit Payments, Supplemental Annuity Payments, and any other benefits payable to the Employee that are considered "divisible" benefits by the Railroad Retirement Board.) The Marital Portion shall be calculated by multiplying such total Non-Tier I benefits by a fraction, the numerator of which is the number of years and months of the Employee's service earned under the Plan during the marriage to the Former Spouse (**from _____ to _____**), and the denominator of which is the Employee's total number of years and months of service earned under the Plan as of his or her date of retirement.

Except for the amount assigned to the Former Spouse above, the Employee shall maintain as his or her **sole and separate property** all other pension benefits that he or she may be eligible to receive from the Railroad Retirement Board based on his or her years of service with a railroad employer.

6. Duration of Payments: The monthly payments under Paragraph 5 shall be paid to the Former Spouse as long as the Employee has the right to receive Railroad Retirement Benefits and shall cease at the death of either party.

7. Overpayments: The Former Spouse agrees that any future overpayments to her or him are recoverable and subject to involuntary collection from her or him or her or his estate.

8. Notification: The Former Spouse agrees to notify the Railroad Retirement Board about any changes in this Qualifying Court Order or the order affecting these provisions of it, or in the eligibility of any recipient receiving benefits pursuant to it.

9. Continued Cooperation of Employee: The Employee agrees to cooperate with the Former Spouse to prepare an application for direct payment to the Former Spouse from the Employee's Railroad Retirement Benefits, if necessary. The Employee agrees to execute all documents that the Railroad Retirement Board may require to certify that the specified portion of the Employee's Railroad Retirement Benefits can be provided to the Former Spouse.

10. Division of Property: The division of Railroad Retirement Benefits in this Order represents a final disposition of property between the Employee and the Former Spouse in compliance with a community property settlement, equitable distribution of property, or other distribution of property that is intended as a present and complete settlement of the property rights of the parties.

11. Jurisdiction: The parties agree that the Court of Common Pleas, Division of Domestic Relations, _____County,_____, is a court of competent jurisdiction in this action. This order bears the certification of _____ of the Court of Common Pleas, Division of Domestic Relations,_____County, _____, and has not been amended, superseded, or set aside by any subsequent order.

12. Qualifying Court Order under the Railroad Retirement Board: The Employee and the Former Spouse intend that this Order qualify under the Railroad Retirement Act, 45 U.S.C. Section 231m. All provisions of this Order shall be construed and/or modified to the extent necessary to conform with the requirements of the Railroad Retirement Board for the division of an Employee's Railroad Retirement Benefits.

13. Merger of Benefits and Indemnification: The Employee agrees not to merge his or her Tier II Railroad Retirement Benefits with any other pension and not to pursue any course of action that would defeat the Former Spouse's right to receive a portion of the Employee's benefits as stipulated herein. The Employee agrees not to take any action by merger of his or her Railroad Retirement pension so as to cause a limitation in the amount of benefits in which the Employee has a vested interest and, therefore, the Employee will not cause a limitation of the Former Spouse's monthly payments as set forth above. The Employee agrees to indemnify Former Spouse for any breach of this paragraph as follows: If the Employee becomes employed or otherwise has his or her Tier II Railroad Retirement Pension merged, which employment or other condition causes a merger of the Employee's Tier II Railroad Retirement Benefits, the Employee will pay to the Former Spouse directly the monthly amount provided in Paragraph 5, under the same terms and conditions as if those payments were made pursuant to the terms of this order.

14. Continued Jurisdiction: The Court retains limited jurisdiction to amend this order for the purposes of maintaining the original intent of the parties and of meeting any requirements to create, conform and maintain this order as a Qualifying Court Order for the division of the Employee's Railroad Retirement Benefits, as stipulated herein. The Court shall also retain jurisdiction to enter such further orders as are necessary to enforce the assignment of benefits to the Former Spouse as set forth herein, including the recharacterization thereof as a division of benefits under another plan, as applicable.

15. Actions by Employee: The Employee shall not take any actions, affirmative or otherwise, that can circumvent the terms and provisions of this Qualified Domestic Relations Order, or that could diminish or extinguish the rights and entitlements of the Former Spouse as set forth herein. Should the Employee take any action or inaction to the detriment of the Former Spouse, he or she shall be required to make sufficient payments directly to the Former Spouse to the extent necessary to neutralize the effects of his or her actions or inactions and to the extent of her or his full entitlements hereunder.

16. Notice of Pending Retirement: The Employee shall be required to notify the Former Spouse, in writing, within thirty (30) days prior to his or her actual date of retirement. Such notice shall indicate his or her intentions to retire and his or her elected benefit commencement date. The notice shall be sent via regular, first class mail. For this purpose, the Former Spouse shall notify the Employee of any changes in her or his mailing address.

CHAPTER 19

Is There Model QDRO Language That You Can Use?

This chapter includes six types of sample QDROs that you may use to secure your interest in your ex-husband's pension or savings plan benefits. It offers three types of sample QDROs for participants covered under defined benefit pension plans and three sample QDROs for use under defined contribution plans, such as 401(k) plans or profit-sharing plans. See Chapter 3 of this book for a discussion of the various types of QDROs and for help in deciding which model QDRO is best for you.

Model QDROs for Defined Benefit Pension Plans

Sample 8:   Separate interest QDRO for active plan participants

Sample 9:   Shared payment QDRO for active plan participants

Sample 10: QDRO for participants who are retired and receiving a monthly pension

Model QDROs for Defined Contribution Plans

Sample 11: QDRO for alternate payees who are assigned 50 percent of the total account balance at the date of divorce

Sample 12: QDRO for alternate payees who are assigned a fixed-dollar amount at the date of divorce

Sample 13: QDRO for alternate payees who are assigned the amounts accumulated during the marriage and the participants had a premarital account balance in the plan before the marriage

SAMPLE 8
SEPARATE INTEREST QDRO FOR DEFINED BENEFIT PENSION PLANS
(For active plan participants)

IT IS HEREBY ORDERED AS FOLLOWS:

1. Effect of this Order as a Qualified Domestic Relations Order: This Order creates and recognizes the existence of an Alternate Payee's right to receive a portion of the Participant's benefits payable under an employer-sponsored defined benefit pension plan that is qualified under Section 401 of the Internal Revenue Code (the "Code") and the Employee Retirement Income Security Act of 1974 ("ERISA"). It is intended to constitute a Qualified Domestic Relations Order ("QDRO") under Section 414(p) of the Code and Section 206(d)(3) of ERISA.

2. Participant Information: The name, last known address, social security number, and date of birth of the plan "Participant" are:

Name: _____

Address: _____

Social Security Number: _____

Date of Birth: _____

3. Alternate Payee Information: The name, last known address, social security number, and date of birth of the "Alternate Payee" are:

Name: _____

Address: _____

Social Security Number: _____

Date of Birth: _____

The Alternate Payee shall have the duty to notify the plan administrator in writing of any changes in her or his mailing address subsequent to the entry of this Order.

4. Plan Name: The name of the Plan to which this Order applies is the _____ (hereinafter referred to as "Plan"). Further, any successor plan to the Plan or any other plan(s), to which liability for provision of the Participant's benefits described below is incurred, shall also be subject to the terms of this Order. Also, any benefits accrued by the Participant under a predecessor plan of the employer or any other defined benefit plan sponsored by the Participant's employer, where liability for benefits accrued under such predecessor plan or other defined benefit plan has been transferred to the Plan, shall also be subject to the terms of this Order.

Any changes in the Plan Administrator, the Plan Sponsor, or the name of the Plan shall not affect the Alternate Payee's rights as stipulated under this Order.

SAMPLE 8 — Continued

5. Pursuant to State Domestic Relations Law: This Order is entered pursuant to the authority granted in the applicable domestic relations laws of the State of _____.

6. For Provision of Marital Property Rights: This Order relates to the provision of marital property rights and/or spousal support to the Alternate Payee as a result of the Order of Divorce between the Participant and the Alternate Payee.

7. Amount of Alternate Payee's Benefit: [Choose A, B, or C]

Alternative A: Coverture Approach

This Order assigns to the Alternate Payee an amount equal to the actuarial equivalent of **Fifty Percent (50%) of the "Marital Portion" of the Participant's accrued benefit** under the Plan as of the Participant's benefit commencement date, or the Alternate Payee's benefit commencement date, if earlier. The Marital Portion of the Participant's accrued benefit shall be determined by multiplying the Participant's accrued benefit by a fraction (less than or equal to 1.0), the numerator of which is the number of months of the Participant's participation in the Plan earned during the marriage (from [*date of marriage*] to [*date of divorce*]), and the denominator of which is the total number of months of the Participant's participation in the Plan as of the earlier of his or her date of cessation of benefit accruals or the date that Alternate Payee commences her or his benefits hereunder.

Alternative B: Percentage Approach

This Order assigns to Alternate Payee an amount equal to the actuarial equivalent of Fifty Percent (50%) of the Participant's accrued benefit under the Plan calculated as of [date of divorce].

Alternative C: Fixed-Dollar Approach

This Order assigns to Alternate Payee a portion of the Participant's accrued benefit under the Plan in an amount equal to $_____ per month, and as may be further adjusted by any actuarial adjustment factors or early commencement reduction factors as set forth in Section 8.

Cost-of-Living Adjustments: In addition to the above, the Alternate Payee shall receive a pro-rata share of any post-retirement **cost of living adjustments** or other economic improvements made to the Participant's benefits on or after the date of his retirement. Such pro-rata share shall be calculated in the same manner as the Alternate Payee's share of the Participant's retirement benefits is calculated pursuant to this Section 7.

8. Commencement Date and Form of Payment to Alternate Payee: The Alternate Payee may elect to commence her or his benefits under the Plan at any time on or after the date the Participant attains the "earliest retirement age" as such term is defined in the Plan and Section 414(p) of the Internal Revenue Code. Further, in the event the Participant becomes eligible to commence benefits at an earlier date as the result of a disability retirement, then the Alternate Payee shall also be entitled to

SAMPLE 8 — Continued

commence her or his share of the benefits at such earlier date. Notwithstanding the above, the Alternate Payee shall commence her or his share of the benefits no later than the Participant's actual date of benefit commencement.

The Alternate Payee may elect to receive her or his benefits in any one of the allowable benefit distribution options permitted under the terms and provisions of the Plan, other than a Qualified Joint & Survivor Annuity with her or his current spouse as the beneficiary.

Separate Interest Approach: This QDRO utilizes a separate interest approach, whereby the Alternate Payee's assigned share of the benefits is to be "actuarially adjusted" to the **life expectancy of such Alternate Payee**. Any actuarial adjustment that may be necessary to convert the Alternate Payee's benefits to her or his own lifetime should be applied to the Alternate Payee's benefits. As a result, should the Participant predecease the Alternate Payee after the Alternate Payee's benefit commencement date, his or her death shall not effect the Alternate Payee's right to continued benefits.

Early Commencement Reductions: Further, should any early commencement reduction be necessary in the event that the Alternate Payee commences benefits prior to the Participant's Normal Retirement Date, then such reduction shall be applied to the Alternate Payee's benefits in accordance with applicable Plan provisions.

Early Retirement Subsidy: Also, the Alternate Payee shall be entitled to a pro rata share of any employer-provided early retirement subsidy provided to the Participant on the date of his or her retirement, and in the event the Alternate Payee has already commenced her or his share of the benefits on the date of the Participant's retirement, then the amounts payable to the Alternate Payee shall be increased in accordance with the Plan Administrator's practices and the Plan's actuarial principles in order to provide the Alternate Payee with a pro rata share of such early retirement subsidy. Such pro rata share shall be calculated in the same manner as the Alternate Payee's share of the Participant's retirement benefits is calculated pursuant to Section 7 of this Order.

Early Retirement Supplements: Further, the Alternate Payee shall be entitled to a pro rata share of any early retirement supplements, interim supplements or temporary benefits that become payable to the Participant that are not considered by the Plan Administrator to be a part of the Participant's accrued benefit as set forth in Section 7. The Alternate Payee's share of such supplemental, interim, or temporary benefits shall be proportional to the Alternate Payee's interest in the Participant's total accrued benefit pursuant to the formula set forth in Section 7.

9. Death of Participant before Benefit Commencement Date: Treatment of Alternate Payee as Surviving Spouse for Purposes of Determining Qualified Preretirement Survivor Annuity as Such Term Is Defined in Section 417 of the Code: In the event that the Participant predeceases the Alternate Payee, and neither the Participant nor the Alternate Payee has commenced its benefits under the Plan, such Alternate Payee shall be designated as the surviving spouse of the Participant for purposes of establishing Alternate Payee's entitlement to receipt of this monthly preretirement survivor annuity, but only to the extent of her or his assigned interest.

SAMPLE 8 — Continued

Participant Required to Maintain Preretirement Survivor Annuity Coverage: In the event that the costs associated with providing this preretirement survivor annuity benefit are not fully subsidized by the Participant's employer, then the Participant must make an affirmative election for such preretirement survivor annuity benefit coverage in a timely manner and in accordance with his or her employer's election procedures. If the Participant terminates his or her employment before retirement, he or she shall still be required to maintain the preretirement survivor annuity coverage in place for the benefit of the Alternate Payee even if the Plan Administrator allows him or her the opportunity to opt out of such coverage. At all times, the Participant shall take whatever steps are necessary in order to maintain the preretirement survivorship coverage in place.

10. Death of Participant after Alternate Payee's Benefit Commencement Date: Pursuant to the terms of Section 8 of this Order, the Alternate Payee's benefits are to be actuarially adjusted to her or his own life expectancy. Under this Separate Interest Approach, once the Alternate Payee commences her or his assigned share of the benefits in accordance with the terms of this Order, the Alternate Payee's right to continued benefits shall be unaffected by the subsequent death of the Participant.

11. Death of Alternate Payee: If the Alternate Payee predeceases the Participant **prior** to the commencement of her or his benefits, the Alternate Payee's portion of Participant's benefits, as stipulated herein, shall become payable to the Alternate Payee's designated beneficiary (or estate), but only to the extent permitted under the terms of the Plan. If the Plan does not permit the Alternate Payee to designate a beneficiary (or estate) for such purposes, then her or his assigned share of the benefits shall revert to the Participant. Should the Alternate Payee predecease the Participant **after** her or his benefit commencement date, then such remaining benefits, if any, will be paid in accordance with the form of benefit elected by such Alternate Payee.

12. Savings Clause: This Order is not intended to, and shall not be construed in such a manner as to, require the Plan:

    (a)   to provide any type or form of benefit option not otherwise provided under the terms of the Plan;

    (b)   to require the Plan to provide increased benefits determined on the basis of actuarial value; or

    (c)   to require the payment of any benefits to the alternate Payee that are required to be paid to another alternate payee under another order that was previously deemed to be a Qualified Domestic Relations Order.

13. Tax Treatment of Distributions Made Under this Order: For purposes of Sections 402(a)(1) and 72 of the Internal Revenue Code, any Alternate Payee who is the spouse or former spouse of the Participant shall be treated as the distributee of any distribution or payments made to the Alternate Payee under the terms of this Order and, as such, will be required to pay the appropriate federal income taxes on such distribution.

14. Constructive Receipt: In the event that the Plan Trustee inadvertently pays to the Participant any benefits that are assigned to the Alternate Payee pursuant to the terms of this Order, the Participant shall immediately reimburse the Alternate Payee to the extent that he or she has received such benefit payments, and shall forthwith pay such amounts so received directly to the Alternate Payee within ten (10) days of receipt.

15. Continued Jurisdiction: The Court shall retain jurisdiction with respect to this Order to the extent required to maintain its qualified status and the original intent of the parties as stipulated herein. The Court shall also retain jurisdiction to enter such further orders as are necessary to enforce the assignment of benefits to the Alternate Payee as set forth herein, including the recharacterization thereof, as a division of benefits under another plan, as applicable, or to make an award of alimony or spousal support, if applicable, in the event that the Participant or the Plan Administrator fail to comply with the provisions contained above requiring said payments to the Alternate Payee.

16. Plan Termination: In the event that the Plan is terminated, whether on a voluntary or involuntary basis, and the Participant's benefits become guaranteed by the Pension Benefit Guaranty Corporation ("PBGC"), the Alternate Payee's benefits, as stipulated herein, shall also be guaranteed to the same extent in accordance with the Plan's termination rules and in the same ratio as the Participant's benefits are guaranteed by the PBGC.

17. Actions by Participant: The Participant shall not take any actions, affirmative or otherwise, that can circumvent the terms and provisions of this Qualified Domestic Relations Order, or that could diminish or extinguish the rights and entitlements of the Alternate Payee as set forth herein. Should the Participant take any action or inaction to the detriment of the Alternate Payee, he or she (or his or her estate) shall be required to make sufficient payments **directly** to the Alternate Payee to the extent necessary to neutralize the effects of his actions or inactions and to the extent of the Alternate Payee's full entitlements hereunder.

18. Notice of Pending Retirement: Pursuant to the terms of Section 8 above, the Alternate Payee shall be required to commence her or his share of the benefits no later than the Participant's actual date of benefit commencement. Therefore, the Participant shall be required to notify the Alternate Payee, in writing, within thirty (30) days prior to his or her actual date of retirement. Such notice shall indicate his or her intentions to retire and his or her elected benefit commencement date. The notice shall be sent via regular, first class mail. For this purpose, the Alternate Payee shall notify the Participant of any changes in her or his mailing address.

IT IS SO ORDERED.

_____

Judge's Signature

SHARED PAYMENT QDRO FOR DEFINED BENEFIT PENSION PLANS
(For active plan participants)

IT IS HEREBY ORDERED AS FOLLOWS:

1. Effect of this Order as a Qualified Domestic Relations Order: This Order creates and recognizes the existence of an Alternate Payee's right to receive a portion of the Participant's benefits payable under an employer-sponsored defined benefit pension plan that is qualified under Section 401 of the Internal Revenue Code (the "Code") and the Employee Retirement Income Security Act of 1974 ("ERISA"). It is intended to constitute a Qualified Domestic Relations Order ("QDRO") under Section 414(p) of the Code and Section 206(d)(3) of ERISA.

2. Participant Information: The name, last known address, social security number, and date of birth of the plan "Participant" are:

Name: _____

Address: _____

Social Security Number: _____

Date of Birth: _____

3. Alternate Payee Information: The name, last known address, social security number, and date of birth of the "Alternate Payee" are:

Name: _____

Address: _____

Social Security Number: _____

Date of Birth: _____

The Alternate Payee shall have the duty to notify the plan administrator in writing of any changes in her or his mailing address subsequent to the entry of this Order.

4. Plan Name: The name of the Plan to which this Order applies is the _____ (hereinafter referred to as "Plan"). Further, any successor plan to the Plan or any other plan(s), to which liability for provision of the Participant's benefits described below is incurred, shall also be subject to the terms of this Order. Also, any benefits accrued by the Participant under a predecessor plan of the employer or any other defined benefit plan sponsored by the Participant's employer, where liability for benefits accrued under such predecessor plan or other defined benefit plan has been transferred to the Plan, shall also be subject to the terms of this Order.

Any changes in the Plan Administrator, the Plan Sponsor, or the name of the Plan shall not affect the Alternate Payee's rights as stipulated under this Order.

SAMPLE 9 — Continued

5. Pursuant to State Domestic Relations Law: This Order is entered pursuant to the authority granted in the applicable domestic relations laws of the State of_____.

6. For Provision of Marital Property Rights: This Order relates to the provision of marital property rights and/or spousal support to the Alternate Payee as a result of the Order of Divorce between the Participant and the Alternate Payee.

7. Amount of Alternate Payee's Benefit: [Choose A, B, or C]

Alternative A: Coverture Approach

This Order assigns to the Alternate Payee an amount equal to **Fifty Percent (50%) of the "Marital Portion" of the Participant's accrued benefit** under the Plan as of the Participant's benefit commencement date. The Marital Portion of the Participant's accrued benefit shall be determined by multiplying the Participant's accrued benefit by a fraction (less than or equal to 1.0), the numerator of which is the number of months of the Participant's participation in the Plan earned during the marriage (from [*date of marriage*] to [*date of divorce*]), and the denominator of which is the total number of months of the Participant's participation in the Plan as of his or her benefit commencement date.

Alternative B: Percentage Approach

This Order assigns to Alternate Payee an amount equal to **Fifty Percent (50%)** of the Participant's accrued benefit under the Plan calculated as of [*date of divorce*].

Alternative C: Fixed-Dollar Approach

This Order assigns to Alternate Payee a portion of the Participant's accrued benefit under the Plan in an amount equal to $_____ per month, and as may be further adjusted by any early commencement reduction factors as set forth in Section 8.

Cost of Living Adjustments: In addition to the above, the Alternate Payee shall receive a pro rata share of any postretirement **cost of living adjustments** or other economic improvements made to the Participant's benefits on or after the date of his or her retirement. Such pro rata share shall be calculated in the same manner as the Alternate Payee's share of the Participant's retirement benefits is calculated pursuant to this Section 7.

8. Commencement Date and Form of Payment to Alternate Payee: The Alternate Payee shall commence her or his assigned share of the benefits when the Participant commences his or her benefits. The Alternate Payee will continue to receive her or his share of the benefits until the earlier to occur of her or his death or the Participant's death.

Shared Payment Approach: This QDRO utilizes the shared payment approach, whereby the Alternate Payee's assigned share of the benefits remains based on the life expectancy of the Participant. As a result, should the Participant predecease the Alternate Payee either before or after his or her benefit commencement date, her or his rights to the benefits assigned to her or him under Section 7 shall cease as of the date of the Participant's death; however, she or he will become entitled to either a qualified preretirement survivor annuity (pursuant to Section 9) or a qualified joint and survivor annuity (pursuant to Section 10), as applicable.

Early Commencement Reductions: Should any **early commencement reduction** be necessary in the event that the Participant and Alternate Payee commence their benefits prior to the Participant's Normal Retirement Date, then they shall each bear their own respective proportional share of the reduction.

Early Retirement Subsidy: The Alternate Payee shall be entitled to a pro rata share of any **early retirement subsidy** provided to the Participant on the date of his retirement. Such pro rata share shall be calculated in the same manner as the Alternate Payee's share of the Participant's retirement benefits is calculated pursuant to Section 7 of this Order.

Early Retirement Supplements: Further, the Alternate Payee shall be entitled to a pro rata share of any early retirement supplements, interim supplements or temporary benefits that become payable to the Participant that are not considered by the Plan Administrator to be a part of the Participant's accrued benefit as set forth in Section 7. The Alternate Payee's share of such supplemental, interim, or temporary benefits shall be proportional to the Alternate Payee's interest in the Participant's total accrued benefit pursuant to the formula set forth in Section 7.

9. Death of Participant before Retirement: Treatment of Alternate Payee as Surviving Spouse for Purposes of Determining Qualified Preretirement Survivor Annuity as Such Term Is Defined in Section 417 of the Code: In the event that the Participant predeceases the Alternate Payee, and neither the Participant nor the Alternate Payee has commenced its benefits under the Plan, such Alternate Payee shall be designated as the surviving spouse of the Participant for purposes of establishing Alternate Payee's entitlement to receipt of this monthly preretirement survivor annuity, but only to the extent of her or his assigned interest as set forth under Section 7.

Participant Required to Maintain Preretirement Survivor Annuity Coverage: In the event that the costs associated with providing this preretirement survivor annuity benefit are not fully subsidized by the Participant's employer, then the Participant must make an affirmative election for such preretirement survivor annuity benefit coverage in a timely manner and in accordance with his or her employer's election procedures. If the Participant terminates his or her employment before retirement, he or she shall still be required to maintain the preretirement survivor annuity coverage in place for the benefit of the Alternate Payee even if the Plan Administrator allows him or her the opportunity to opt out of such coverage. At all times, the Participant shall take whatever steps are necessary to maintain the preretirement survivorship coverage in place.

10. Death of Participant after Retirement: Treatment of Alternate Payee as Surviving Spouse for Purposes of Determining Qualified (Postretirement) Joint and Survivor Annuity as Such Term is Defined in Section 417 of the Code: In the event that the Participant predeceases the Alternate Payee after his or her date of retirement, such Alternate Payee shall be designated as the surviving spouse of the Participant for purposes of establishing the Alternate Payee's entitlement to receipt of this monthly postretirement survivor annuity, but only to the extent of her or his assigned interest as set forth under Section 7.

Participant Required to Elect Benefit in the Form of a 50 Percent Qualified Joint and Survivor Annuity: Upon the Participant's retirement, he or she shall be required to elect his or her benefit in the form of a 50 percent joint and survivor annuity. Should the Participant predecease the Alternate Payee after retirement, she or he will receive a portion of the (postretirement) survivor annuity to the extent of her or his assigned interest. Any eligible subsequent spouse of the Participant may receive the remainder of any survivor annuity benefits above and beyond those payable to the Alternate Payee. Notwithstanding the above, if the Participant is not remarried on the date of his or her retirement, the Alternate Payee shall receive any and all (postretirement) survivor annuity benefits that may become payable under the Plan on the Participant's death.

11. Death of Alternate Payee: If the Alternate Payee predeceases the Participant **either prior to or after** her or his commencement of benefits, the Alternate Payee's portion of the Participant's benefits, as stipulated herein, shall revert to the Participant.

12. Savings Clause: This Order is not intended to, and shall not be construed in such a manner as to, require the Plan:

    (a)   to provide any type or form of benefit option not otherwise provided under the terms of the Plan;

    (b)   to require the Plan to provide increased benefits determined on the basis of actuarial value; or

    (c)   to require the payment of any benefits to the alternate Payee that are required to be paid to another alternate payee under another order that was previously deemed to be a Qualified Domestic Relations Order.

13. Tax Treatment of Distributions Made under this Order: For purposes of Sections 402(a)(1) and 72 of the Internal Revenue Code, any Alternate Payee who is the spouse or former spouse of the Participant shall be treated as the distributee of any distribution or payments made to the Alternate Payee under the terms of this Order and, as such, will be required to pay the appropriate federal income taxes on such distribution.

14. Constructive Receipt: In the event that the Plan Trustee inadvertently pays to the Participant any benefits that are assigned to the Alternate Payee pursuant to the terms of this Order, the Participant shall immediately reimburse the Alternate Payee to the extent that he or she has received such benefit payments, and shall forthwith pay such amounts so received directly to the Alternate Payee within ten (10) days of receipt.

15. Continued Jurisdiction: The Court shall retain jurisdiction with respect to this Order to the extent required to maintain its qualified status and the original intent of the parties as stipulated herein. The Court shall also retain jurisdiction to enter such further orders as are necessary to enforce the assignment of benefits to the Alternate Payee as set forth herein, including the recharacterization thereof, as a division of benefits under another plan, as applicable, or to make an award of alimony or spousal support, if applicable, in the event that the Participant or the Plan Administrator fail to comply with the provisions contained above requiring said payments to the Alternate Payee.

16. Plan Termination: In the event that the Plan is terminated, whether on a voluntary or involuntary basis, and the Participant's benefits become guaranteed by the Pension Benefit Guaranty Corporation ("PBGC"), the Alternate Payee's benefits, as stipulated herein, shall also be guaranteed to the same extent in accordance with the Plan's termination rules and in the same ratio as the Participant's benefits are guaranteed by the PBGC.

17. Actions by Participant: The Participant shall not take any actions, affirmative or otherwise, that can circumvent the terms and provisions of this Qualified Domestic Relations Order, or that could diminish or extinguish the rights and entitlements of the Alternate Payee as set forth herein. Should the Participant take any action or inaction to the detriment of the Alternate Payee, he or she (or his or her estate) shall be required to make sufficient payments **directly** to the Alternate Payee to the extent necessary to neutralize the effects of his or her actions or inactions and to the extent of the Alternate Payee's full entitlements hereunder.

18. Notice of Pending Retirement: Pursuant to the terms of Section 8, the Alternate Payee shall commence her or his share of the benefits when the Participant commences his or her benefits. Therefore, the Participant shall be required to notify the Alternate Payee, in writing, within thirty (30) days prior to his or her actual date of retirement. Such notice shall indicate his or her intentions to retire and his or her elected benefit commencement date. The notice shall be sent via regular, first class mail. For this purpose, the Alternate Payee shall notify the Participant of any changes in her or his mailing address.

IT IS SO ORDERED.

_____
Judge's Signature

SAMPLE 10
PARTICIPANT ALREADY RETIRED IN A DEFINED BENEFIT PENSION PLAN
(Utilizing fixed-dollar award and providing entire survivor annuity to alternate payee based on election at retirement)

IT IS HEREBY ORDERED AS FOLLOWS:

1. Effect of this Order as a Qualified Domestic Relations Order: This Order creates and recognizes the existence of an Alternate Payee's right to receive a portion of the Participant's benefits payable under an employer-sponsored defined benefit pension plan that is qualified under Section 401 of the Internal Revenue Code (the "Code") and the Employee Retirement Income Security Act of 1974 ("ERISA"). It is intended to constitute a Qualified Domestic Relations Order ("QDRO") under Section 414(p) of the Code and Section 206(d)(3) of ERISA.

2. Participant Information: The name, last known address, social security number, and date of birth of the plan "Participant" are:

Name: _____

Address: _____

Social Security Number: _____

Date of Birth: _____

3. Alternate Payee Information: The name, last known address, social security number, and date of birth of the "Alternate Payee" are:

Name: _____

Address: _____

Social Security Number: _____

Date of Birth: _____

The Alternate Payee shall have the duty to notify the plan administrator in writing of any changes in her or his mailing address subsequent to the entry of this Order.

4. Plan Name: The name of the Plan to which this Order applies is the _____ (hereinafter referred to as "Plan"). Further, any successor plan to the Plan or any other plan(s), to which liability for provision of the Participant's benefits described below is incurred, shall also be subject to the terms of this Order. Also, any benefits accrued by the Participant under a predecessor plan of the employer or any other defined benefit plan sponsored by the Participant's employer, where liability for benefits accrued under such predecessor plan or other defined benefit plan has been transferred to the Plan, shall also be subject to the terms of this Order.

SAMPLE 10 — Continued

Any changes in the Plan Administrator, the Plan Sponsor, or the name of the Plan shall not affect the Alternate Payee's rights as stipulated under this Order.

5. Pursuant to State Domestic Relations Law: This Order is entered pursuant to the authority granted in the applicable domestic relations laws of the State of _____.

6. For Provision of Marital Property Rights: This Order relates to the provision of marital property rights and/or spousal support to the Alternate Payee as a result of the Order of Divorce between the Participant and the Alternate Payee.

7. Amount of Alternate Payee's Benefit and Duration of Payments: From the benefits otherwise payable to the Participant each month, this Order assigns to Alternate Payee an amount equal to $ _____ per month commencing _____ [*first of month following submission of QDRO to plan administrator*: remember, this date must be on a prospective basis]. The Alternate Payee shall continue to receive her or his assigned share of the benefits as set forth in this Section 7, until the earlier to occur of her or his death or the Participant's death. However, should the Participant predecease the Alternate Payee, she or he shall then become entitled to a postretirement survivor annuity as set forth in section 8.

8. Death of Participant: Treatment of Alternate Payee as Surviving Spouse for Purposes of Determining Qualified Joint and Survivor Annuity as Such Term Is Defined in Section 417 of the Code: In the event that the Participant predeceases the Alternate Payee, such Alternate Payee shall be designated as the surviving spouse of the Participant for purposes of establishing Alternate Payee's entitlement to receipt of this entire monthly postretirement survivor annuity as elected by the Participant when he or she retired. For purposes of determining the eligibility for such surviving spouse benefits, the Alternate Payee and the Participant have satisfied the one (1) year marriage requirement as enumerated in Sections 401(a)(11) and 417(d) of the Code and as may be required under the provisions of the Plan.

9. Death of Alternate Payee: If the Alternate Payee predeceases the Participant, the Alternate Payee's assigned share of the benefits, as stipulated herein, shall revert to the Participant.

10. Savings Clause: This Order is not intended to, and shall not be construed in such a manner as to, require the Plan:

(a) to provide any type or form of benefit option not otherwise provided under the terms of the Plan;

(b) to require the Plan to provide increased benefits determined on the basis of actuarial value; or

(c) to require the payment of any benefits to the alternate Payee that are required to be paid to another alternate payee under another order that was previously deemed to be a Qualified Domestic Relations Order.

11. Tax Treatment of Distributions Made under this Order: For the purposes of Sections 402(a)(1) and 72 of the Internal Revenue Code, any Alternate Payee who is the spouse or former spouse of the Participant shall be treated as the distributee of any distribution or payments made to the Alternate Payee under the terms of this Order and, as such, will be required to pay the appropriate federal income taxes on such distribution.

12. Constructive Receipt: In the event that the Plan Trustee inadvertently pays to the Participant any benefits that are assigned to the Alternate Payee pursuant to the terms of this Order, the Participant shall immediately reimburse the Alternate Payee to the extent that he or she has received such benefit payments, and shall forthwith pay such amounts so received directly to the Alternate Payee within ten (10) days of receipt.

13. Continued Jurisdiction: The Court shall retain jurisdiction with respect to this Order to the extent required to maintain its qualified status and the original intent of the parties as stipulated herein. The Court shall also retain jurisdiction to enter such further orders as are necessary to enforce the assignment of benefits to the Alternate Payee as set forth herein, including the recharacterization thereof, as a division of benefits under another plan, as applicable, or to make an award of alimony or spousal support, if applicable, in the event that the Participant or Plan Administrator fail to comply with the provisions contained above requiring said payments to the Alternate Payee.

14. Plan Termination: In the event that the Plan is terminated, whether on a voluntary or involuntary basis, and the Participant's benefits become guaranteed by the Pension Benefit Guaranty Corporation ("PBGC"), the Alternate Payee's benefits, as stipulated herein, shall also be guaranteed to the same extent in accordance with the Plan's termination rules and in the same ratio as the Participant's benefits are guaranteed by the PBGC.

15. Actions by Participant: The Participant shall not take any actions, affirmative or otherwise, that can circumvent the terms and provisions of this Qualified Domestic Relations Order, or that could diminish or extinguish the rights and entitlements of the Alternate Payee as set forth herein. Should the Participant take any action or inaction to the detriment of the Alternate Payee, he or she (or his or her estate) shall be required to make sufficient payments **directly** to the Alternate Payee to the extent necessary to neutralize the effects of his or her actions or inactions and to the extent of the Alternate Payee's full entitlements hereunder.

IT IS SO ORDERED.

_____
Judge's Signature

SAMPLE 11
DEFINED CONTRIBUTION PLANS
(For use when simply assigning 50 percent of total account balance)

IT IS HEREBY ORDERED AS FOLLOWS:

1. Effect of this Order as a Qualified Domestic Relations Order: This Order creates and recognizes the existence of an Alternate Payee's right to receive a portion of the Participant's benefits payable under an employer-sponsored defined contribution plan that is qualified under Section 401 of the Internal Revenue Code (the "Code") and the Employee Retirement Income Security Act of 1974 ("ERISA"). It is intended to constitute a Qualified Domestic Relations Order ("QDRO") under Section 414(p) of the Code and Section 206(d)(3) of ERISA.

2. Participant Information: The name, last known address, social security number, and date of birth of the plan "Participant" are:

Name: _____

Address: _____

Social Security Number: _____

Date of Birth:_____

3. Alternate Payee Information: The name, last known address, social security number, and date of birth of the "Alternate Payee" are:

Name: _____

Address: _____

Social Security Number: _____

Date of Birth:_____

The Alternate Payee shall have the duty to notify the Plan Administrator in writing of any changes in his or her mailing address subsequent to the entry of this Order.

4. Plan Name: The name of the Plan to which this Order applies is the _____

(hereinafter referred to as "Plan"). Any changes in Plan Administrator, Plan Sponsor, or the name of the Plan shall not affect the Alternate Payee's rights as stipulated under this Order.

5. Pursuant to State Domestic Relations Law: This Order is entered pursuant to the authority granted in the applicable domestic relations laws of the State of _____.

6. For Provision of Marital Property Rights: This Order relates to the provision of marital property rights and/or spousal support to the Alternate Payee as a result of the Order of Divorce between the Participant and the Alternate Payee.

7. Amount of Alternate Payee's Benefit: This Order assigns to Alternate Payee an amount equal to **Fifty Percent (50%)** of the Participant's Total Account Balance accumulated under the Plan as of [*date of divorce*] (or the closest valuation date thereto), plus any interest and investment earnings or losses attributable thereon for periods subsequent to [*date of divorce*], until the date of total distribution. Further, such Total Account Balance shall include all amounts maintained under all of the various accounts and/or subaccounts established on behalf of the Participant. Further, such Account Balance shall include all amounts (including plan forfeitures, if applicable) contributed to the Plan on behalf of the Participant after [*date of divorce*], that are attributable to periods prior to such date. The Alternate Payee's share of the benefits shall be allocated on a pro rata basis among all of the accounts and/or investment funds maintained on behalf of the Participant under the Plan.

In the event the Alternate Payee does not elect an immediate distribution, her or his share of the benefits described above shall be **segregated and separately maintained** in account(s) established on her or his behalf and shall additionally be credited with any interest and investment income or losses attributable thereon from [*date of divorce*], until the date of total distribution to the Alternate Payee.

8. Commencement Date and Form of Payment to Alternate Payee: If the Alternate Payee so elects, she or he shall be paid her or his benefits as soon as administratively feasible following the date this Order is approved as a Qualified Domestic Relations Order by the Plan Administrator, or at the earliest date permitted under the Plan or Section 414(p) of the Internal Revenue Code, if later. Benefits will be payable to the Alternate Payee in any form or permissible option otherwise available to participants and alternate payees under the terms of the Plan, including, but not limited to, a single lump sum cash payment.

9. Alternate Payee's Rights and Privileges: On and after the date that this Order is deemed to be a Qualified Domestic Relations Order, but before the Alternate Payee receives her or his total distribution under the Plan, the Alternate Payee shall be entitled to all of the rights and election privileges that are afforded to Plan beneficiaries, including, but not limited to, the rules regarding the right to designate a beneficiary for death benefit purposes and the right to direct Plan investments, only to the extent permitted under the provisions of the Plan.

10. Death of Alternate Payee: In the event of the Alternate Payee's death prior to the Alternate Payee receiving the full amount of benefits called for under this Order and under the benefit option chosen by the Alternate Payee, such Alternate Payee's beneficiary(ies), as designated on the appropriate form provided by the Plan Administrator (or, in the absence of a beneficiary designation, her or his estate), shall receive the remainder of any unpaid benefits under the terms of this Order.

11. Death of Participant: In the event that the Participant dies **prior** to the establishment of separate account(s) in the name of the Alternate Payee, such Alternate Payee shall be treated as the surviving spouse of the Participant for any death benefits payable under the Plan to the extent of the full amount of her or his benefits as called for under Paragraph 7 of this Order. Should the Participant predecease the Alternate Payee **after** the new account(s) have been established on her or his behalf, such Participant's death shall not affect the Alternate Payee's rights to receive her or his assigned portion of the benefits as set forth herein.

12. Savings Clause: This Order is not intended to, and shall not be construed in such a manner as to, require the Plan:

(a) to provide any type or form of benefit option not otherwise provided under the terms of the Plan;

(b) to require the Plan to provide increased benefits determined on the basis of actuarial value; or

(c) to require the payment of any benefits to the Alternate Payee that are required to be paid to another alternate payee under another order that was previously deemed to be a Qualified Domestic Relations Order.

13. Tax Treatment of Distributions Made under this Order: For the purposes of Sections 402(a)(1) and 72 of the Internal Revenue Code, any Alternate Payee who is the spouse or former spouse of the Participant shall be treated as the distributee of any distribution or payments made to the Alternate Payee under the terms of this Order and, as such, will be required to pay the appropriate federal income taxes on such distribution.

14. Constructive Receipt: In the event that the Plan Trustee inadvertently pays to the Participant any benefits that are assigned to the Alternate Payee pursuant to the terms of this Order, the Participant shall immediately reimburse the Alternate Payee to the extent that he or she has received such benefit payments, and shall forthwith pay such amounts so received directly to the Alternate Payee within ten (10) days of receipt.

15. Continued Jurisdiction: The Court shall retain jurisdiction with respect to this Order to the extent required to maintain its qualified status and the original intent of the parties as stipulated herein. The Court shall also retain jurisdiction to enter such further orders as are necessary to enforce the assignment of benefits to the Alternate Payee as set forth herein, including the recharacterization thereof as a division of benefits under another plan, as applicable, or to make an award of alimony, if applicable, in the event that the Participant fails to comply with the provisions contained above requiring said payments to the Alternate Payee.

16. Plan Termination: In the event of a Plan termination, the Alternate Payee shall be entitled to receive her or his portion of the Participant's benefits as stipulated herein in accordance with the Plan's termination provisions for participants and beneficiaries.

17. Actions by Participant: The Participant shall not take any actions, affirmative or otherwise, that can circumvent the terms and provisions of this Qualified Domestic Relations Order, or that could diminish or extinguish the rights and entitlements of the Alternate Payee as set forth herein. Should the Participant take any action or inaction to the detriment of the Alternate Payee, he or she shall be required to make sufficient payments directly to the Alternate Payee to the extent necessary to neutralize the effects of his or her actions or inactions and to the extent of her or his full entitlements hereunder.

IT IS SO ORDERED.

_____
Judge's Signature

SAMPLE 12
DEFINED CONTRIBUTION PLANS
(For use when assigning a fixed-dollar amount)

IT IS HEREBY ORDERED AS FOLLOWS:

1. Effect of this Order as a Qualified Domestic Relations Order: This Order creates and recognizes the existence of an Alternate Payee's right to receive a portion of the Participant's benefits payable under an employer-sponsored defined contribution plan that is qualified under Section 401 of the Internal Revenue Code (the "Code") and the Employee Retirement Income Security Act of 1974 ("ERISA"). It is intended to constitute a Qualified Domestic Relations Order ("QDRO") under Section 414(p) of the Code and Section 206(d)(3) of ERISA.

2. Participant Information: The name, last known address, social security number, and date of birth of the plan "Participant" are:

Name: _____

Address: _____

Social Security Number: _____

Date of Birth: _____

3. Alternate Payee Information: The name, last known address, social security number, and date of birth of the "Alternate Payee" are:

Name: _____

Address: _____

Social Security Number: _____

Date of Birth: _____

The Alternate Payee shall have the duty to notify the Plan Administrator in writing of any changes in his or her mailing address subsequent to the entry of this Order.

4. Plan Name: The name of the Plan to which this Order applies is the _____

(hereinafter referred to as "Plan"). Any changes in the Plan Administrator, the Plan Sponsor, or the name of the Plan shall not affect the Alternate Payee's rights as stipulated under this Order.

5. Pursuant to State Domestic Relations Law: This Order is entered pursuant to the authority granted in the applicable domestic relations laws of the State of _____.

6. For Provision of Marital Property Rights: This Order relates to the provision of marital property rights and/or spousal support to the Alternate Payee as a result of the Order of Divorce between the Participant and the Alternate Payee.

7. Amount of Alternate Payee's Benefit: This Order assigns to Alternate Payee a portion of Participant's Total Account Balance under the Plan in an amount equal to $ _____, effective as of [*date of divorce*] (or the closest valuation date thereto), plus any interest and investment earnings or losses attributable thereon for periods subsequent to [*date of divorce*], until the date of total distribution. The Alternate Payee's share of the benefits shall be allocated on a pro rata basis among all of the accounts and/or investment funds maintained on behalf of the Participant under the Plan.

In the event the Alternate Payee does not elect an immediate distribution, her or his share of the benefits described above shall be **segregated and separately maintained** in account(s) established on her or his behalf and shall additionally be credited with any interest and investment income or losses attributable thereon from [*date of divorce*], until the date of total distribution to the Alternate Payee.

8. Commencement Date and Form of Payment to Alternate Payee: If the Alternate Payee so elects, she or he shall be paid her or his benefits as soon as administratively feasible following the date this Order is approved as a Qualified Domestic Relations Order by the Plan Administrator, or at the earliest date permitted under the Plan or Section 414(p) of the Internal Revenue Code, if later. Benefits will be payable to the Alternate Payee in any form or permissible option otherwise available to participants and alternate payee's under the terms of the Plan, including, but not limited to, a single lump sum cash payment.

9. Alternate Payee's Rights and Privileges: On and after the date that this Order is deemed to be a Qualified Domestic Relations Order, but before the Alternate Payee receives her or his total distribution under the Plan, the Alternate Payee shall be entitled to all of the rights and election privileges that are afforded to Plan beneficiaries, including, but not limited to, the rules regarding the right to designate a beneficiary for death benefit purposes and the right to direct Plan investments, only to the extent permitted under the provisions of the Plan.

10. Death of Alternate Payee: In the event of the Alternate Payee's death prior to the Alternate Payee receiving the full amount of benefits called for under this Order and under the benefit option chosen by the Alternate Payee, such Alternate Payee's beneficiary(ies), as designated on the appropriate form provided by the Plan Administrator (or, in the absence of a beneficiary designation, her or his estate), shall receive the remainder of any unpaid benefits under the terms of this Order.

11. Death of Participant: In the event that the Participant dies **prior** to the establishment of separate account(s) in the name of the Alternate Payee, such Alternate Payee shall be treated as the surviving spouse of the Participant for any death benefits payable under the Plan to the extent of the full amount of her or his benefits as called for under Paragraph 7 of this Order. Should the Participant predecease the Alternate Payee **after** the new account(s) have been established on her or his behalf, such Participant's death shall not affect the Alternate Payee's rights to receive her or his assigned portion of the benefits as set forth herein.

12. Savings Clause: This Order is not intended to, and shall not be construed in such a manner as to, require the Plan:

    (a)   to provide any type or form of benefit option not otherwise provided under the terms of the Plan;

    (b)   to require the Plan to provide increased benefits determined on the basis of actuarial value; or

    (c)   to require the payment of any benefits to the Alternate Payee which are required to be paid to another alternate payee under another order which was previously deemed to be a Qualified Domestic Relations Order.

13. Tax Treatment of Distributions Made under this Order: For the purposes of Sections 402(a)(1) and 72 of the Internal Revenue Code, any Alternate Payee who is the spouse or former spouse of the Participant shall be treated as the distributee of any distribution or payments made to the Alternate Payee under the terms of this Order and, as such, will be required to pay the appropriate federal income taxes on such distribution.

14. Constructive Receipt: In the event that the Plan Trustee inadvertently pays to the Participant any benefits which are assigned to the Alternate Payee pursuant to the terms of this Order, the Participant shall immediately reimburse the Alternate Payee to the extent that he or she has received such benefit payments, and shall forthwith pay such amounts so received directly to the Alternate Payee within ten (10) days of receipt.

15. Continued Jurisdiction: The Court shall retain jurisdiction with respect to this Order to the extent required to maintain its qualified status and the original intent of the parties as stipulated herein. The Court shall also retain jurisdiction to enter such further orders as are necessary to enforce the assignment of benefits to the Alternate Payee as set forth herein, including the recharacterization thereof as a division of benefits under another plan, as applicable, or to make an award of alimony, if applicable, in the event that the Participant fails to comply with the provisions contained above requiring said payments to the Alternate Payee.

16. Plan Termination: In the event of a Plan termination, the Alternate Payee shall be entitled to receive her or his portion of the Participant's benefits as stipulated herein in accordance with the Plan's termination provisions for participants and beneficiaries.

17. Actions by Participant: The Participant shall not take any actions, affirmative or otherwise, that can circumvent the terms and provisions of this Qualified Domestic Relations Order, or that could diminish or extinguish the rights and entitlements of the Alternate Payee as set forth herein. Should the Participant take any action or inaction to the detriment of the Alternate Payee, he or she shall be required to make sufficient payments **directly** to the Alternate Payee to the extent necessary to neutralize the effects of his or her actions or inactions and to the extent of her or his full entitlements hereunder.

IT IS SO ORDERED.

_____

Judge's Signature

SAMPLE 13
DEFINED CONTRIBUTION PLANS
(For use when participant keeps premarital account balance*)

IT IS HEREBY ORDERED AS FOLLOWS:

1. Effect of this Order as a Qualified Domestic Relations Order: This Order creates and recognizes the existence of an Alternate Payee's right to receive a portion of the Participant's benefits payable under an employer-sponsored defined contribution plan that is qualified under Section 401 of the Internal Revenue Code (the "Code") and the Employee Retirement Income Security Act of 1974 ("ERISA"). It is intended to constitute a Qualified Domestic Relations Order ("QDRO") under Section 414(p) of the Code and Section 206(d)(3) of ERISA.

2. Participant Information: The name, last known address, social security number, and date of birth of the plan "Participant" are:

Name: _____

Address: _____

Social Security Number: _____

Date of Birth: _____

3. Alternate Payee Information: The name, last known address, social security number, and date of birth of the "Alternate Payee" are:

Name: _____

Address: _____

Social Security Number: _____

Date of Birth: _____

The Alternate Payee shall have the duty to notify the Plan Administrator in writing of any changes in his or her mailing address subsequent to the entry of this Order.

4. Plan Name: The name of the Plan to which this Order applies is the _____ (hereinafter referred to as "Plan"). Any changes in the Plan Administrator, the Plan Sponsor, or the name of the Plan shall not affect the Alternate Payee's rights as stipulated under this Order.

5. Pursuant to State Domestic Relations Law: This Order is entered pursuant to the authority granted in the applicable domestic relations laws of the State of_____.

6. For Provision of Marital Property Rights: This Order relates to the provision of marital property rights and/or spousal support to the Alternate Payee as a result of the Order of Divorce between the Participant and the Alternate Payee.

---

*NOTE: This model QDRO essentially provides the alternate payee with fifty percent (50%) of the difference between the account balance on the date of divorce and the account balance on the date of marriage.

SAMPLE 13 — Continued

7. Amount of Alternate Payee's Benefit: This Order assigns to Alternate Payee a portion of the Participant's Total Account Balance under the Plan equal to **Fifty Percent (50%)** of [(a) *MINUS* (b)] below, where:

    (a)   equals the Participant's Total Account Balance accumulated under the Plan as of [*date of divorce*] (or the closest valuation date thereto); and

    (b)   equals the Participant's Total Account Balance accumulated under the Plan as of [*date of marriage*] (or the closest valuation date thereto).

The Alternate Payee's share of the benefits shall be allocated on a pro rata basis among all of the accounts and/or investment funds maintained on behalf of the Participant under the Plan.

Additionally, the Alternate Payee's assigned share of the benefits shall include any interest and investment earnings or losses attributable thereon for periods subsequent to [*date of divorce*], until the date of total distribution.

In the event the Alternate Payee does not elect an immediate distribution, her or his share of the benefits described above shall be **segregated and separately maintained** in account(s) established on her or his behalf and shall additionally be credited with any interest and investment income or losses attributable thereon from [*date of divorce*], until the date of total distribution to the Alternate Payee.

8. Commencement Date and Form of Payment to Alternate Payee: If the Alternate Payee so elects, she or he shall be paid her or his benefits as soon as administratively feasible following the date this Order is approved as a Qualified Domestic Relations Order by the Plan Administrator, or at the earliest date permitted under the Plan or Section 414(p) of the Internal Revenue Code, if later. Benefits will be payable to the Alternate Payee in any form or permissible option otherwise available to participants and alternate payees under the terms of the Plan, including, but not limited to, a single lump sum cash payment.

9. Alternate Payee's Rights and Privileges: On and after the date that this Order is deemed to be a Qualified Domestic Relations Order, but before the Alternate Payee receives her or his total distribution under the Plan, the Alternate Payee shall be entitled to all of the rights and election privileges that are afforded to Plan beneficiaries, including, but not limited to, the rules regarding the right to designate a beneficiary for death benefit purposes and the right to direct Plan investments, only to the extent permitted under the provisions of the Plan.

10. Death of Alternate Payee: In the event of the Alternate Payee's death prior to the Alternate Payee receiving the full amount of benefits called for under this Order and under the benefit option chosen by the Alternate Payee, such Alternate Payee's beneficiary(ies), as designated on the appropriate form provided by the Plan Administrator (or, in the absence of a beneficiary designation, her or his estate), shall receive the remainder of any unpaid benefits under the terms of this Order.

11. Death of Participant: In the event that the Participant dies **prior** to the establishment of separate account(s) in the name of the Alternate Payee, such Alternate Payee shall be treated as the surviving spouse of the Participant for any death benefits payable under the Plan to the extent of the full amount of her or his benefits as called for under Paragraph 7 of this Order. Should the Participant predecease the Alternate Payee **after** the new account(s) have been established on her or his behalf, such Participant's death shall not affect the Alternate Payee's rights to receive her or his assigned portion of the benefits as set forth herein.

12. Savings Clause: This Order is not intended to, and shall not be construed in such a manner as to, require the Plan:

(a) to provide any type or form of benefit option not otherwise provided under the terms of the Plan;

(b) to require the Plan to provide increased benefits determined on the basis of actuarial value; or

(c) to require the payment of any benefits to the Alternate Payee that are required to be paid to another alternate payee under another order that was previously deemed to be a Qualified Domestic Relations Order.

13. Tax Treatment of Distributions Made under this Order: For the purposes of Sections 402(a)(1) and 72 of the Internal Revenue Code, any Alternate Payee who is the spouse or former spouse of the Participant shall be treated as the distributee of any distribution or payments made to the Alternate Payee under the terms of this Order and, as such, will be required to pay the appropriate federal income taxes on such distribution.

14. Constructive Receipt: In the event that the Plan Trustee inadvertently pays to the Participant any benefits that are assigned to the Alternate Payee pursuant to the terms of this Order, the Participant shall immediately reimburse the Alternate Payee to the extent that he or she has received such benefit payments, and shall forthwith pay such amounts so received directly to the Alternate Payee within ten (10) days of receipt.

15. Continued Jurisdiction: The Court shall retain jurisdiction with respect to this Order to the extent required to maintain its qualified status and the original intent of the parties as stipulated herein. The Court shall also retain jurisdiction to enter such further orders as are necessary to enforce the assignment of benefits to the Alternate Payee as set forth herein, including the recharacterization thereof as a division of benefits under another plan, as applicable, or to make an award of alimony, if applicable, in the event that the Participant fails to comply with the provisions contained above requiring said payments to the Alternate Payee.

16. Plan Termination: In the event of a Plan termination, the Alternate Payee shall be entitled to receive her or his portion of the Participant's benefits as stipulated herein in accordance with the Plan's termination provisions for participants and beneficiaries.

17. Actions by Participant: The Participant shall not take any actions, affirmative or otherwise, that can circumvent the terms and provisions of this Qualified Domestic Relations Order, or that could diminish or extinguish the rights and entitlements of the Alternate Payee as set forth herein. Should the Participant take any action or inaction to the detriment of the Alternate Payee, he or she shall be required to make sufficient payments **directly** to the Alternate Payee to the extent necessary to neutralize the effects of his or her actions or inactions and to the extent of her or his full entitlements hereunder.

IT IS SO ORDERED.

_____

Judge's Signature

GLOSSARY
QDRO and Pension Terminology

This glossary includes some common terms associated with pension plans and the QDRO process. It's not mandatory reading, but you may want to become familiar with some of these terms if you are pursuing the QDRO yourself or if you want to take a proactive approach with your attorney.

Account balance: A participant's benefits under a defined contribution plan. A participant's total account balance under a plan may consist of amounts established and maintained under various subaccounts. For example, a plan may contain pretax and after-tax employee contribution accounts and employer-match accounts. Further, each subaccount may contain various investment fund alternatives in which a participant may choose to invest contributions.

Accrued benefit: The amount of benefits a plan participant has accumulated or accrued as of a particular date, generally based on the employee's actual years of service with the company and average earnings calculated as of such date. This term is normally used only in conjunction with defined benefit pension plans and indicates the amount of unreduced benefits a participant is entitled to receive at the employee's normal retirement date.

Actuarial equivalent: The actuarial adjustment necessary to convert a participant's benefits into different forms and/or payment periods so that the total value of a participant's pension benefits remains equal (on an actuarial basis), regardless of the form of benefit or the commencement date the participant may elect.

Actuarial reduction: The actuarial adjustment required when a plan participant elects to commence pension benefits before normal retirement age. Because the participant's benefits will commence before normal retirement age, they must be reduced on the basis of the participant's life expectancy and the fact that the individual will be receiving benefits over a longer period of time. Under a defined benefit pension plan, a participant's projected accrued benefit is predetermined on the basis of a specific formula and is calculated to commence on an unreduced basis at normal retirement age. Actuarial reductions may also be required when converting a life-only benefit to another form of benefit, such as a qualified joint or survivor annuity.

Alternate payee: Any spouse, former spouse, child, or other dependent of a participant who is recognized by a domestic relations order as having a right to receive all, or a portion of, the benefits payable under a plan with respect to such participant.

Annuity: A series of periodic payments made over a specified period of time. Most defined benefit pension plans provide lifetime annuities for plan participants. Under a QDRO, an alternate payee may receive an actuarially adjusted lifetime annuity based on her or his own life expectancy. Generally, a defined contribution plan, such as a 401(k) plan, provides benefits only in the form of a lump sum distribution. Some, however, do provide lifetime annuities or an annuity payable for a certain period (installment payments).

Anti-circumvention language: Anti-circumvention language refers to those sections of a separation agreement, judgment entry, or QDRO that protect the rights of the former spouse against actions taken by the participant to her or his detriment. Participants may attempt to circumvent the provisions of a separation agreement or QDRO by taking some action that will limit or extinguish the ex-spouse's rights to a portion of the pension. For example, a participant may terminate his employment and request a refund of employee contributions rather than provide his former spouse with a portion of the retirement annuity. With proper anti-circumvention language, the participant will be required to provide payments directly to the former spouse if he or she takes such an action that will affect her or his rights and entitlements.

Beneficiary: A person or persons designated by a participant to receive pension benefits in the event of his or her death. Certain defined benefit pension plans provide annuities whereby only a surviving spouse (or an alternate payee under a QDRO) is eligible for continued benefits in the event of the participant's death. Quite often, though, these plans allow optional forms of benefits under which participants may name a beneficiary other than a spouse.

Benefit multiplier: Under many union and other hourly rated defined benefit plans, a participant's pension benefits are not related to salary. The plan document contains a benefit multiplier to determine the participant's accrued benefit as of any point in time. For example, the accrued benefit may incorporate a benefit multiplier of $30 per month per year of service. In this manner, for employees retiring with 25 years of service, their monthly annuity will equal $750 per month (25 years x $30). The use of a benefit multiplier rather than average salary provides a convenient method for unions to negotiate members' pension benefits.

COAP (**court order acceptable for processing**): A court order accepted by the Civil Service Retirement System (CSRS) and the Federal Employees Retirement System (FERS) for the purpose of dividing a participant's federal pension benefits. Because the federal government is exempt from ERISA's QDRO provisions, the court order should not be referred to as a QDRO. All COAPS should be sent to the Office of Personnel Management (OPM) in Washington, DC, for processing.

Cost of living adjustment (COLA): COLA is a plan provision that allows a pension to keep pace with inflation. Most government plans have provisions allowing the plan to increase each year in response to changes in inflation. Typically, the consumer price index (CPI) is used as the measuring stick for COLAS. COLAS may be either compounding or noncompounding. Compounding COLAS are more attractive because the yearly increase is based on the preceding year, but noncompounding COLA adjustments are always predicated on the original year.

Coverture approach: The recommended approach for equitably dividing benefits under a defined benefit pension plan. The former spouse's 50 percent share of the benefit is based on the participant's accrued benefit determined as of his or her date of retirement. The accrued benefit is then multiplied by a coverture fraction, the numerator of which is equal to the service earned by the participant during the marriage, and the denominator of which is equal to his or her total service under the plan. The former spouse would then receive 50 percent of this coverture percentage. This method provides the former spouse with inflationary protection on her or his ownership share of the pension. It does not freeze her or his 50 percent share as of the date of divorce.

Deferred vested participant: An employee who terminates employment with a company after satisfying the plan's vesting requirements and thus becomes entitled to receive the vested accrued benefit accumulated as of the date of termination. A deferred vested participant must normally defer commencement of benefits until reaching normal retirement age as defined under the plan (usually age 65). At that time, the participant will be entitled to commence the vested accrued benefit on an unreduced basis. Many pension plans allow a deferred vested participant to commence benefits on an actuarially reduced basis once the participant meets the plan's age requirement for early retirement.

Defined benefit pension plan: A pension plan qualified under ERISA and the IRC that provides a specific predeterminable amount of benefits to a participant at that individual's projected date of retirement. Normally, the benefits are based on a formula that incorporates the participant's projected years of service and final average compensation. Defined benefit plans are required to be funded on an ongoing basis in accordance with actuarial principles enumerated in ERISA and the IRC. A participant's benefits under a defined benefit pension plan are referred to as accrued benefits.

Defined contribution plan: A plan qualified under ERISA and the IRC that provides for contributions directly to individual accounts established and maintained for each plan participant. The contributions may consist of either employee or employer contributions, or both. The participant is generally entitled to receive the account balance (together with any interest accrued thereon as well as investment gains and/or losses) when the employee retires or otherwise terminates employment with the company. There are several types of defined contribution plans, including profit-sharing plans, thrift plans, 401(k) plans, retirement savings plans, stock bonus plans, and employee stock ownership plans (ESOPs).

Department of Labor (DOL): Many provisions of ERISA are administered by the Department of Labor. The DOL issues opinion letters and requires certain information to be completed by plan sponsors.

Domestic relations order: Any judgment, decree, or order (including approval of a property settlement agreement) that (1) relates to the provision of child support, alimony payments, or marital property rights to a spouse, former spouse, child, or other dependent of a participant, and (2) is made pursuant to a state domestic relations law (including a community property law).

Earliest retirement age: The age at which a plan participant may first begin receiving pension benefits under the provisions of the plan. Normally, benefits payable to someone before normal retirement age are actuarially reduced to reflect the earlier commencement of benefits. For QDRO purposes, the term means the earlier of: (1) the date on which the participant is entitled to a distribution under the plan, or (2) the later of: (a) the date the participant attains age 50, or (b) the earliest date on which the participant could begin receiving benefits under the plan if the participant separated from service.

Early retirement subsidy: A benefit provided to an early retiree (someone who commences pension benefits before normal retirement age) that has not been actuarially reduced to reflect such early commencement of benefits. The employer is, in effect, subsidizing the participant's pension benefit to the extent that it exceeds what would otherwise have been payable with a full actuarial reduction.

Fiduciary: With respect to pension plans, persons who exercise discretionary authority or discretionary control concerning the management of the plan or disposition of its assets.

Final average compensation: One of the components often found under an ERISA-governed defined benefit pension plan. It usually represents the average of a plan participant's compensation earned during the final years of his or her employment, when his or her salary is the highest. Typically, it is the average compensation over a period of three or five consecutive years, when the participant's compensation was the highest.

IRA: An individual retirement account that may be established by people for the purpose of deferring the tax on a portion of their income. Tax-deductible contributions may be made to an IRA each year, up to a specified maximum. This is a good vehicle for people who are not covered under any employer-sponsored retirement program. Many employees establish IRAs for the purpose of rolling over distributions they receive under their employers' pension and profit-sharing plans. Any amounts that are directly transferred to an IRA are tax-deferred, and the company making the plan distribution does not automatically withhold 20 percent of the distribution for federal income tax purposes.

IRC: Internal Revenue Code of 1986, as amended. This is the basic federal tax law governing all employees and qualified retirement programs. IRC Section 414(p) contains the provisions for QDROs.

Lump sum distribution: A type of distribution made under a qualified retirement plan. Employees or retirees receiving a lump sum distribution may take advantage of certain favorable tax treatment, such as forward averaging, when computing the level of income tax that is due.

Matching employer contributions: Contributions made by the employer to a defined contribution benefit plan, such as a 401(k) retirement savings plan, based on a certain percentage of the employee's own contribution. For example, an employer may contribute 50 cents on the dollar for each dollar an employee contributes to the plan on a payroll deduction basis, up to 6 percent of his or her base salary. An employee may become fully vested in his or her matching employer contributions immediately or may be subject to a vesting schedule based on the employee's years of service.

Merger of benefits: It may be possible for participants covered under a pension plan to merge their previous service or credits earned under another retirement system into the current plan. For example, civil servants may merge their benefits earned under the military into their federal civil service pension. When preparing a QDRO or court order to divide pension benefits, consider other benefits that participants may have earned under another retirement system.

Pension Benefit Guaranty Corporation (PBGC): The government agency established to insure employer-sponsored pension plans that terminate with unfunded liability. Title IV of ERISA contains information relative to the establishment and functions of the PBGC. The PBGC maintains an Interest Rate Hotline, (202) 326-4041, that provides the interest rates for valuing annuity benefits in single-employer and multiemployer plans.

Qualified Domestic Relations Order (QDRO): A domestic relations order issued by a state court that creates or recognizes the right of an alternate payee to receive all or a portion of the pension benefits payable with respect to a plan participant. In order to be a QDRO, it must satisfy the criteria enumerated in Section 414(p) of the Internal Revenue Code, as amended. Plan administrators have total discretionary authority to determine whether a QDRO satisfies such requirements.

Qualified Joint and Survivor Annuity (QJSA): A form of benefit available under a defined benefit pension plan and sometimes found in defined contribution plans in which benefit payments continue after the death of the plan participant to the surviving spouse, if any. Typically, the amount of benefit that continues to the surviving spouse is anywhere from 50 percent to 100 percent of the benefit the participant had been receiving before death. Upon the death of the surviving spouse, all benefit payments cease. Because this form of benefit provides pension payments that extend beyond the death of the plan participant, the monthly benefit payments made while the participant is alive are actuarially reduced to account for the potentially longer stream of benefit payments. This actuarial reduction takes into account the life expectancy of the surviving spouse in addition to the life expectancy of the plan participant.

Qualified Preretirement Survivor Annuity (QPSA): A form of death benefit normally payable under a defined benefit pension plan to the surviving spouse of an active employee (or a deferred vested participant) who is vested under the plan but dies before the commencement of retirement benefits. This benefit is normally calculated as if the plan participant had survived to the earliest retirement age and then died with a 50 percent qualified joint and survivor annuity election in place.

Summary plan description (SPD): A written description of an employee benefit plan that must be furnished to all plan participants under an ERISA-governed employee benefit plan. The purpose of this ERISA-required summary is to provide plan participants with summaries of the employer's various benefit plan documents clear and concise language that the average plan participant can understand.

Ten-year-certain-and-continuous form of benefit payment: A form of benefit payment that can be found in many defined benefit pension plans. When a participant commences his or her benefits under this form, they are payable on a reduced basis for the remainder of his or her lifetime, with the proviso that should he or she die before 120 monthly payments have been made, then the remainder of such 120 monthly payments shall be made to his or her designated beneficiary. The benefits are slightly reduced to reflect the added risk associated with the probability that the participant will die before receiving 120 monthly payments.

Tier I of Railroad Pension: The Social Security component of Railroad Retirement Act pensions. Typically, it is calculated in the same way as a Social Security benefit. Tier I benefits are not divisible by court order.

Tier II of Railroad Pension: The second level of benefits under the Railroad Retirement Act. The benefit is determined by multiplying the participant's average monthly earnings for the highest five years, using the Tier II tax base, by the number of years of service. This amount is then multiplied by 0.7 percent to determine the monthly benefit. For example, a railroad retiree with 30 years of service and average monthly earnings of $3,000 would receive a Tier II monthly annuity of $630 ($3,000 x 30 years x 0.007%). The Railroad Retirement Board will honor a court order to divide Tier II benefits.

Vested benefits: The portion of a participant's accrued benefit that is nonforfeitable. Vesting is based on the participant's years of service under the plan. For plans that adopt the five-year schedule, all participants become 100 percent vested after five years of service. Until then, their vesting percentage is zero. Some plans contain *graded* vesting schedules, whereby participants' vesting percentage increases each year until they become 100 percent vested. Under federal law, employers who use a graded vesting schedule must provide full vesting after seven years of service. Government pension plans and multiemployer plans may adopt an even longer vesting schedule.